Crypto Essentials Book Four

Building Wealth with Crypto Trading and Investing Strategies

Scott Jenkins

Tigress Publishing

Disclaimer

The information contained in this book is provided for educational and informational purposes only. While every effort has been made to ensure that the information provided is accurate and up to date, the author makes no warranties, either express or implied, regarding the completeness, reliability, or accuracy of the content.

Readers should not rely solely on the information provided in this book when making financial, legal, or investment decisions. The content is not intended to serve as professional advice and should not replace consultation with a licensed expert in fields such as financial planning, investing, law, or any other professional services.

By using the information contained in this book, the reader agrees that the author is not liable for any losses, damages, or inconveniences incurred, either directly or indirectly, as a result of the use or misuse of the content provided, including but not limited to errors, omissions, or inaccuracies.

Always do your own research and consult with a qualified professional before making any decisions based on the information in this book. Cryptocurrency markets are volatile and involve significant risk, and individual results may vary.

Contents

Contents

Introduction

IMAGINE WAKING UP ONE day to discover that your carefully planned investments have not only secured your financial future but also provided the freedom to pursue your passions without worry. This dream is becoming a reality for many who master the art of cryptocurrency trading and investing. Take Jeffrey Harvey, a senior at Arizona State University majoring in social media and mass communication. Jeffrey invested in cryptocurrencies and when there was a pump in the market in November 2024, he took 30 percent of his profits and bought a camper van in which he plans to travel the country and make podcasts (NY Post). Stories like Jeffrey's highlight the transformative power of crypto strategies tailored to a fast-paced, ever-evolving market.

This book, "***Crypto Essentials Book Four: Building Wealth with Crypto Trading and Investing Strategies***," is about more than just profits; it's about empowerment. It's about equipping you with the tools and knowledge to confidently navigate the complexities of the cryptocurrency market while focusing on strategies that ensure long-term success. Whether you're just starting your trading journey or looking to refine your investment approach, this book provides actionable insights designed for the modern crypto enthusiast.

The Journey So Far

In ***Crypto Essentials Book One: Understanding the Fundamentals of Cryptocurrencies and Blockchain Technologies***, we began by laying the foundational principles of cryptocurrency and blockchain technology. In ***Crypto Essentials Book Two: A Comprehensive Guide to the Acronyms and Key Terms***, we delved into the terminology and introduced readers to decentralized finance (DeFi). In ***Crypto Essentials Book Three: Getting Started with Trading and Investing Cryptocurrencies***, we guided you through the practical steps of setting up accounts on crypto exchanges, securing wallets, and taking those crucial first steps in the crypto world. To learn more about each book, scan the QR code below

Crypto Essentials Book Series

Now, ***Crypto Essentials Book Four*** takes the baton. We're shifting gears to focus on the strategies and techniques that can turn a functional knowledge of crypto into tangible wealth-building opportunities. If you've ever wondered how to make sense of market trends, use technical tools effectively, or create a robust portfolio, you're in the right place.

The Objectives of This Book

This book is designed to:

1. Break down the complexities of trading and investing strategies into digestible, actionable steps.

2. Provide practical techniques for managing risk and maximizing returns in a volatile market.

3. Highlight the importance of building confidence and maintaining discipline in trading decisions.

4. Equip readers with the mindset and tools needed to achieve sustainable financial growth.

5. Use real-world examples to illustrate strategies, making the concepts relatable and applicable.

By focusing on these objectives, this book ensures you're not just informed but empowered to take control of your financial future.

What You'll Learn

Here's a sneak peek of what lies ahead:

1. Understanding Market Narratives: Learn how to identify and adapt to the evolving trends that drive the crypto space.

2. Trading Techniques for Success: From technical analysis to identifying market patterns, we'll cover the essentials that help traders make informed decisions.

3. Investment Strategies for Long-Term Growth: Explore the benefits of diversification, staking, and yield farming to build a robust portfolio.

4. Mastering Risk Management: Protect your capital with tools and techniques that minimize losses while maximizing gains.

A Fresh Approach

This book emphasizes the importance of adapting to the ever-changing nature of crypto markets. Viral trends, emerging tokens, and shifting market sentiments can redefine the landscape overnight. Whether it's a meme coin taking off on TikTok or a new DeFi protocol capturing investor attention, staying informed and flexible is critical.

This dynamic environment underscores the need for due diligence. DYOR (Do Your Own Research) remains a cornerstone of success in crypto investing. While this book provides a structured guide, your ability to critically evaluate and adapt to new information will ultimately determine your success.

The Path Ahead

The chapters ahead are crafted to equip you with everything you need to navigate the crypto market with confidence and clarity. From understanding market dynamics to implementing practical strategies, this book is your companion on the journey to building wealth through crypto trading and investing.

Let's dive in and unlock the potential of the cryptocurrency market together.

Chapter One

Building the Right Mindset for Crypto Trading Success

THE WORLD OF CRYPTOCURRENCY trading is fast-paced, exhilarating, and at times, overwhelming. If you've ever made an impulsive trade in response to a surge in market excitement or a sharp drop in prices, you've probably experienced firsthand how emotions can shape investment decisions. While technical analysis, trading strategies, and market research are undeniably important, the psychological component of trading often plays an even more pivotal role in determining long-term success.

Understanding the Psychology of Trading

Consider the case of Tom, an enthusiastic young investor who jumped into the crypto market during a sudden bull run. The hype around Bitcoin's meteoric rise convinced him that he had found a surefire path to quick wealth. Eager to capitalize on the upward momentum, he made a large investment, convinced that the market would continue to soar. But within a few days, Bitcoin experienced a sharp correction, and Tom's portfolio took a heavy hit.

Despite the loss, Tom couldn't help but feel that he had missed out. Determined to recover, he doubled down on his investments, chasing after even higher returns. Unfortunately, this emotional decision led him further down the rabbit hole of impulsive trading, as the market fluctuations began to control his decisions. Tom's story, though hypothetical, is a reflection of a pattern seen all too often in the crypto world: emotional investing.

The Link between Psychology and Trading

In trading, as in life, emotions are a double-edged sword. On one hand, emotions like excitement and confidence can drive us to make bold decisions. On the other hand, negative emotions like fear, greed, and anxiety can cloud our judgment, leading to impulsive or poorly timed trades. This psychological battle is particularly pronounced in the crypto space, where the markets are volatile, and price swings can be dramatic.

Understanding the psychology of trading is essential for building a successful long-term strategy. No matter how much you study technical analysis or market trends, if you are not in control of your emotions, you may find yourself making decisions that undermine your financial goals.

Emotional Management: The Key to Staying in Control

Crypto trading is not just about numbers; it's about managing your emotions. Emotional management, or the ability to remain calm, collected, and rational in the face of market fluctuations, is one of the most valuable skills you can develop as a trader. It's the difference between making a calculated decision and reacting impulsively to market noise.

When we're emotionally attached to our investments, it can cloud our judgment. For instance, after witnessing a sharp price drop, fear may prompt us to sell prematurely, locking in losses instead of waiting for the market to recover. Similarly, after seeing profits soar, we may succumb to greed, leading us to make risky trades without fully understanding the risks involved.

A successful trader needs to be able to manage their emotions, especially during market volatility. One of the most important aspects of emotional management is developing a clear trading plan and sticking to it (more to follow on this in future chapters). This plan should include rules about entry and exit points, stop-loss orders, and risk management strategies. When you have a well-thought-out plan, it becomes easier to avoid making rash decisions in the heat of the moment.

Additionally, accepting the inherent volatility of crypto markets is a crucial part of emotional management. Crypto markets are known for their swings, and no trader can predict every movement with certainty. By learning to embrace this volatility rather than fear it, you can reduce the emotional stress that comes with price fluctuations.

Discipline: A Trader's Best Friend

Discipline is another core element of a trader's psychological toolkit. It involves sticking to your strategy, even when market conditions make it tempting to deviate. One of the primary reasons traders fail is their inability to follow a consistent strategy. They might abandon their plan when the market is experiencing a short-term rally or sell off too quickly during a downturn, driven by the urge to "do something."

Tom's story from earlier is a classic example of lack of discipline. Instead of following a systematic approach, he let fear and greed guide his decisions, which ultimately led to greater losses. This scenario can be avoided by developing and committing to a disciplined approach.

The Importance of Mindset Over Technical Skills

While technical skills—such as reading price charts, using technical indicators, and understanding market cycles—are undeniably important in crypto trading, your mindset will ultimately determine whether you succeed or fail. In fact, many experienced traders argue that mindset is the most important factor in achieving consistent profits. While technical skills can be learned and improved over time, cultivating the right mindset requires self-awareness, practice, and emotional regulation.

The world of crypto is constantly shifting, and even the most knowledgeable traders can experience losses. It's your mindset that allows you to weather these storms, stay focused on your long-term goals, and avoid making emotionally driven decisions.

A growth mindset is essential for any trader. This is the belief that your abilities can improve with effort and learning. When you adopt a growth mindset, you're more likely to view mistakes as opportunities for learning, rather than as failures. In the context of crypto trading, this means understanding that losses are part of the process and using them to refine your strategies.

Benefits of Emotional Detachment from Trades

One of the hallmarks of successful traders is their ability to detach emotionally from their trades. This doesn't mean they don't care about their investments; rather, it means they can make decisions based on logic and analysis, rather than emotional reactions.

Emotional detachment offers several key benefits:

1. **Reduced Stress:** By not letting emotions govern your trades, you can approach each decision with a calm, clear mind. This can help you avoid the stress and anxiety that comes with market fluctuations.

2. **Fewer Impulsive Decisions:** When you're emotionally detached, you're less likely to chase after the latest trend or make trades based on fear of missing out (FOMO). Instead, you'll rely on a systematic approach to your trades, ensuring consistency and control.

3. **Better Risk Management:** Emotional detachment allows you to assess risks more rationally. You're more likely to stick to your stop-loss orders and avoid putting your capital in risky, high-re-

ward investments without conducting thorough research.

4. **Improved Decision-Making:** Without the cloud of emotions, your ability to make well-reasoned, informed decisions improves dramatically. You'll be better equipped to evaluate opportunities and make trades that align with your long-term strategy.

Balancing Ambition with Risk Awareness

While ambition and the desire to grow your portfolio are important driving factors in trading, they must be tempered with a realistic understanding of the risks involved. In the fast-moving world of cryptocurrency, it's easy to get swept up in the excitement of potential profits, but it is essential to balance this ambition with a healthy sense of caution.

Inexperienced traders often become overly ambitious, hoping to strike it rich in a short period. However, as Tom's story illustrates, untempered ambition can lead to impulsive decisions and significant losses. To strike the right balance, you need to set realistic goals, focus on consistent, incremental gains, and always be aware of the risks involved in each trade.

Risk management is an integral part of balancing ambition and risk. This includes strategies such as setting stop-loss orders, diversifying your portfolio, and never investing more than you can afford to lose. By incorporating these measures into your strategy, you can pursue your ambition to grow your wealth while mitigating the potential for catastrophic losses.

Developing Patience: The Secret to Long-Term Success

The final psychological trait that all successful traders share is patience. It's easy to get caught up in the excitement of a rapidly changing market, but true success in crypto trading comes from taking a step back and focusing on the long term.

Crypto markets are often described as being volatile, and that's an understatement. Prices can swing drastically within a matter of hours, and while it's tempting to act on these short-term movements, doing so without a clear strategy often leads to losses. Successful traders understand that, just as in any investment, patience pays off.

Having patience means allowing your trades to develop over time. It means resisting the urge to sell after a short-term dip and trusting in your long-term strategy. It's about being able to hold through the ups and downs, knowing that the best opportunities often require time to unfold.

Overcoming Fear, Greed, and FOMO (Fear of Missing Out)

In the fast-paced world of cryptocurrency trading, the psychological triggers of fear, greed, and FOMO often drive traders to make decisions that go against their best interests. These emotions can cloud judgment and lead to impulsive actions, such as buying high or selling low, causing unnecessary losses. In this section, we will delve into strategies for managing these emotions, identifying emotional triggers, and techniques for avoiding impulsive decisions.

Strategies for Managing Fear, Greed, and FOMO

It's impossible to eliminate fear, greed, and FOMO completely from the trading experience. These emotions are deeply ingrained in human psychology and are natural reactions to market volatility. However, what differentiates successful traders from the unsuccessful ones is their ability to manage these emotions rather than allowing them to take control.

Fear: Understanding its Role in Trading

Fear is perhaps the most common emotion experienced by traders, particularly in highly volatile markets like crypto. Fear of losing money, fear of missing out on profits, and even fear of the unknown can cause traders to make irrational decisions.

- **Fear of Losing Money**: In crypto trading, the fear of losing your hard-earned capital can cause hesitation, leading to missed opportunities or premature sell-offs.

- **Fear of Missing Out (FOMO)**: FOMO often arises when you see others profiting from a trade you didn't enter, or when the price of a coin skyrockets. The fear of missing out on potential gains can compel traders to act impulsively.

- **Fear of the Unknown**: The crypto market is new and relatively unregulated, which can cause uncertainty. This fear can lead to conservative or erratic behavior, as traders seek safety in predictability.

Managing fear involves accepting loss as part of the game. Successful traders understand that it's impossible to win every trade and that losses are not a reflection of failure but rather a learning experience. They take calculated risks and rely on solid risk management strategies.

A great way to manage fear is to predefine your risk for each trade. Before entering a position, decide how much you're willing to lose (this is often referred to as your "stop-loss"), and stick to it. Knowing that you've already set your parameters can significantly reduce the fear of losing.

Greed: Keeping Ambition in Check

Greed is the counterpart to fear, and while it can be a motivator, it can also derail your trading journey. When greed takes over, traders become obsessed with making larger profits, often at the cost of sound risk management practices.

Greed may manifest in a few ways:

- **Overleveraging**: Betting too much capital on one position with the hopes of a large return.

- **Chasing Profits**: Continuously entering the market with the desire for more, without considering the inherent risks.

- **Holding Too Long**: Greedy traders often hold onto assets for too long, hoping for a bigger gain, only to watch the price fall dramatically.

To combat greed, it's essential to establish clear profit-taking rules. Decide on an exit strategy for each trade, whether it's a specific price target, a percentage gain, or a set timeframe. When you reach your profit goal, take your profits and move on. Avoid the temptation to hold onto trades for longer than necessary in hopes of further price increases.

Greed can also be mitigated by focusing on consistent, incremental gains rather than trying to hit a home run with each trade. This long-term perspective encourages a more measured approach to trading, reducing the impact of greed on decision-making.

FOMO: Recognizing the Trap

FOMO is a trader's Achilles' heel. It's what drives people to make emotional decisions based on market movements rather than sound analysis. FOMO can cause traders to jump into trades after a massive price surge, hoping to ride the wave but often buying at the peak. The sudden market downturn that follows leaves them holding the (empty) bag.

FOMO is particularly pervasive in crypto markets, where price surges can happen rapidly, often fueled by social media trends, celebrity endorsements, or viral news stories. As traders see prices rising and others profiting, they feel the urge to act quickly before they're left behind.

The FOMO cycle often looks like this:

1. The price of an asset starts to rise quickly.
2. News spreads, and social media amplifies the excitement.
3. You start to feel like you're missing out, even though you didn't plan to buy.

4. In an attempt to not "miss the boat," you enter the market at a high price.

5. The price inevitably corrects, leaving you with a loss.

Identifying Emotional Triggers

The first step in overcoming fear, greed, and FOMO is self-awareness — knowing when these emotions are influencing your trading decisions. Every trader has emotional triggers, moments when emotions like fear or greed begin to dictate their actions.

Fear Triggers:

- A sudden market dip or flash crash.
- Watching your portfolio drop in value, especially after a recent high.
- News of an exchange hack or a regulatory crackdown on cryptocurrency.

Solution: Practice mindfulness and take a step back. Rather than reacting immediately, take time to process the situation calmly. Avoid making decisions based on panic or the desire to "fix" the situation.

Greed Triggers:

- Seeing others make significant profits from a particular trade.
- The idea of hitting a "home run" by betting heavily on one asset.
- The desire for more when you've already achieved a reasonable

profit.

Solution: Develop and stick to a profit-taking strategy. Recognize when you've made enough for the day or week and be satisfied with smaller, consistent gains. Greed thrives when there is a fear of missing out on the next opportunity, so remind yourself that there will always be more opportunities.

FOMO Triggers:

- Seeing a crypto asset shoot up in value on social media or news sites.
- Watching a token being talked about by influencers or celebrities.
- Peer pressure from other traders, especially in group chats or online communities.

Solution: Acknowledge that FOMO is a natural emotional response but also a destructive one. Instead of immediately jumping into a trade, pause and assess if it aligns with your trading plan and strategy. Consider whether the price increase is driven by fundamentals or merely speculative hype.

Techniques to Avoid Impulsive Buying/Selling

Now that we've examined how to recognize emotional triggers, the next step is to implement techniques that help avoid impulsive buying and selling. These strategies will help you make more rational decisions in the heat of the moment and keep you from making moves that could harm your portfolio in the long run.

Implementing a Trading Plan

One of the most effective ways to avoid impulsive decisions is to choose and stick with a well-defined trading plan. A trading plan serves as a roadmap, outlining your entry and exit points, stop-loss orders, risk tolerance, and profit-taking strategy. When you are tempted to make a snap decision based on emotions, your trading plan should act as a reminder of the strategy you've committed to.

A good trading plan includes:

- **Entry Rules:** Clearly define when to enter a trade based on specific conditions, such as technical indicators or fundamental news.

- **Exit Rules:** Set your target prices for profits and loss limits to prevent emotional selling or buying.

- **Risk Management:** Never risk more than a fixed percentage of your portfolio on any single trade.

Setting Stop-Loss Orders

A stop-loss order is one of the best tools to prevent impulsive selling. By predefining your exit point at a certain loss level, you automatically remove the emotion from the process. When the price hits your stop-loss, your trade is closed automatically, preventing you from holding onto a losing position out of fear or denial.

Similarly, take-profit orders work the same way—automating the sale of an asset once it reaches your desired profit. This helps you avoid the temptation to hold on for more gains, which can lead to unnecessary risk if the market reverses.

Setting Time-Based Rules

Time-based rules can also help combat impulsive behavior. For example, you might decide not to make any trades during periods of high volatility, or you might limit yourself to only entering trades after conducting a set amount of research.

Taking breaks from the market can also help clear your mind and reduce the emotional weight of the market's movements. For instance, if you find yourself glued to the screen during a price surge, consider stepping away for a set amount of time to allow yourself to gain a fresh perspective.

Using a Paper Trading Account

If you're new to trading or struggling with impulsive decisions, a paper trading account can be a great way to practice emotional control without risking real money. These accounts simulate real market conditions and allow you to make trades using virtual funds. While you won't experience the financial consequences, it can help you build discipline and practice sticking to your trading plan.

Developing a Long-Term Vision

In the crypto world, it's easy to get caught up in the allure of quick profits. Stories of people becoming overnight millionaires–especially during periods of rapid bull runs, flood social media and news outlets, enticing many traders to take the plunge in hopes of hitting it big. However, the reality is that while the potential for short-term gains exists, the most successful crypto traders and investors are those who adopt a long-term vision. Focusing on sustainability and growth rather than immediate profits helps mitigate the emotional highs and lows of the market and sets the stage for a more consistent path to success.

Benefits of Focusing on Sustainability and Growth Rather Than Short-Term Gains

While quick profits can certainly be tempting, they are not the most reliable strategy for long-term wealth accumulation. Short-term trading, driven by impulsive decisions and emotional reactions to market movements, often leads to more volatility and risk. This type of trading can be stressful, unpredictable, and ultimately, unsustainable.

Instead, focusing on a long-term vision allows you to ride out the inevitable ups and downs of the crypto market. The benefits of this approach include:

- Reduced emotional stress – Short-term trading often leads to emotional exhaustion. The constant need to monitor price movements and make snap decisions can result in anxiety, (FOMO), and frustration, especially when things don't go according to plan. In contrast, a long-term approach allows you to detach from daily price fluctuations, giving you peace of mind. When you're focused on the bigger picture, short-term volatility is much less stressful.

- More rational decision making – focusing on long-term goals encourages a more rational decision-making process. Rather than being swayed by market noise or the fear of missing out on a hot trend, long-term investors make decisions based on fundamentals—such as the use case, team, and technological potential of a cryptocurrency—rather than emotional impulses. This results in more disciplined trading and investing, which leads to better long-term outcomes.

- Compound growth over time – one of the most powerful benefits of taking a long-term approach is the potential for compound growth. By focusing on sustainability and reinvesting profits over time, your assets can grow exponentially. This is particularly relevant in the crypto world, where the underlying technology—such as decentralized finance (DeFi), staking, and yield farming—offers opportunities to earn passive income.

- Enhanced portfolio stability– a long-term perspective allows you to diversify your portfolio and build a balanced mix of assets. Spreading your investments across stable assets (e.g., Bitcoin, Ethereum, or stablecoins) and promising altcoins, helps to reduce your exposure to the volatility of any single asset. This diversified approach will better withstand market corrections and improve the overall stability of your portfolio.

- Alignment with real-world innovation –crypto isn't just about trading tokens; it's about investing in transformative technologies that are reshaping the world. A long-term approach allows you to align your investments with the real-world applications of blockchain technology. Whether it's decentralized finance (DeFi), smart contracts, or blockchain-based supply chains, understanding and investing in the technology's potential can provide both financial returns and satisfaction as you support projects that have the potential to make a lasting impact.

Case Study: "Maximizing Gains with Long-Term Holding"

Let's take the story of Tim Draper, a well-known venture capitalist and early Bitcoin investor. In 2014, Draper made headlines when he purchased 30,000 Bitcoins for just $19 million in a U.S. government auction of seized Bitcoin. At the time, Bitcoin was priced at around $600 per coin, and the cryptocurrency market was still in its early stages. Many saw Bitcoin as a speculative asset, and skepticism was high regarding its long-term viability.

However, Draper saw the potential for Bitcoin to revolutionize financial systems globally, so he held onto his investment, despite the market's volatility and the frequent downturns. Over the years, Draper's patience paid off. By 2017, Bitcoin had surpassed $20,000 during its bull run, by 2021, Bitcoin reached over $60,000 and in December 2024, it reached the $100,000 mark.

Draper's initial $19 million investment in Bitcoin had grown to over $1.8 billion by 2021. His success story illustrates the power of long-term commitment and conviction in the crypto market, even when the market is volatile and sentiment is uncertain. Draper didn't sell during the bear markets or fear the wild price swings; he remained confident in Bitcoin's technology and its future potential.

This story highlights the value of holding through volatility and sticking to a long-term strategy. Like Draper, many early investors who held through the highs and lows of the market ultimately reaped the rewards of their patience.

Chapter Two

Crypto Market Fundamentals

THE CRYPTOCURRENCY MARKET IS known for its volatility and its seemingly unpredictable price movements. However, if you look closely, you'll notice a recurring trend that has played a significant role in shaping major crypto trends: the four-year cycle. This cycle, largely influenced by Bitcoin's halving events, has become a cornerstone of market sentiment and is a key factor in understanding the ebb and flow of crypto prices.

Understanding Market Sentiment and Trends

Consider the story of Jessica, a seasoned crypto trader who learned the importance of timing through experience. In 2017, when Bitcoin was riding high and hitting new all-time highs, Jessica was cautious. Instead of following the hype and jumping in at the peak, she remembered the pattern from previous cycles. Bitcoin's halving event was just around the corner, and based on her knowledge of the four-year cycle, Jessica anticipated a pullback before another major surge.

Jessica patiently waited through the market correction in early 2018, dollar cost averaging (DCA) into Bitcoin whilst the price was still low, and by the time Bitcoin entered its next bull phase in 2020, she was positioned to capitalize on the gains. By following the pattern and making strategic decisions based on historical trends, Jessica not only grew her portfolio but also reinforced her belief in the power of market cycles.

This story is a perfect example of how understanding market sentiment and the cyclical nature of the crypto market can enable you to make more informed, strategic decisions. In this section, we'll dive into the four-year cycle, how it connects to Bitcoin's halving events, and how understanding this cycle can help you navigate the crypto market.

Crypto Four-Year Cycle Overview

One of the most fascinating and influential concepts in the cryptocurrency market is the four-year cycle. This cycle is primarily driven by Bitcoin's halving events, which occur approximately every four years. Bitcoin's halving refers to the process by which the reward for mining new blocks is cut in half. This event reduces the rate at which new bitcoins are created and released to the market, and thus lowers the rate of inflation in the market.

The halving events are significant because they directly impact the supply of Bitcoin, and supply and demand is a fundamental driver of price movements in any market. With fewer new Bitcoins being mined after each halving, the available supply is reduced while demand typically increases as more people become aware of Bitcoin's potential as a store of value and an investment asset.

The four-year cycle can be broken down into distinct phases, each one contributing to the overall sentiment and trends of the market. Let's explore how this cycle unfolds and how it shapes the broader crypto market.

The Connection Between Bitcoin's Halving and Market Sentiment

Bitcoin's halving events are typically the catalyst for the four-year cycle, and understanding their impact on market sentiment is key to identifying future trends.

1. **Pre-Halving Phase**: In the lead-up to the halving event, Bitcoin tends to experience a bullish rally as investors anticipate the reduced supply of new coins. The market becomes more optimistic, and this often drives prices higher as demand increases in response to the upcoming halving.

2. **Post-Halving Phase**: After the halving occurs, there is often a period of consolidation as the market adjusts to the new supply dynamics. The reduced inflation rate can lead to an increase in long-term confidence in Bitcoin's price stability, but the immediate effect may not always be dramatic.

3. **Bull Market Phase**: As the effects of the halving take hold, Bitcoin's price usually begins to rise significantly over the next 12 months, as the reduced supply and sustained demand drive up the value. This is often the phase where mass adoption and media

attention begin to ramp up, and more mainstream investors enter the market, further fueling the bull run.

4. **Bear Market Phase**: After the bullish peak, the market often experiences a correction, or even a prolonged bear market, as profits are taken and confidence begins to wane. Prices can drop significantly, but the long-term trend is typically upward as the cycle prepares to begin again.

Crypto Four-Year Cycle

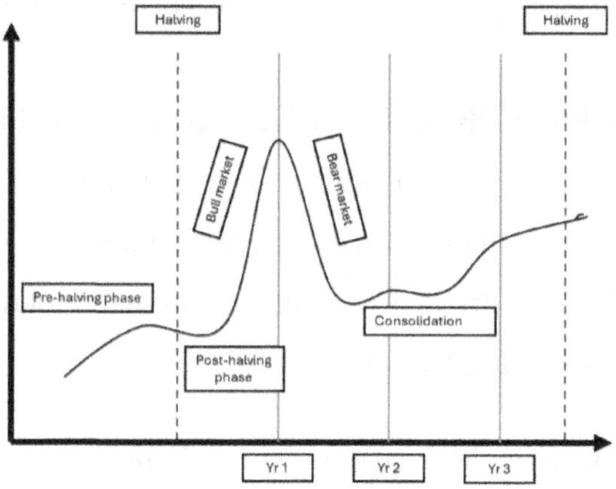

The Halving and Its Historical Price Movements (2013-2017, 2017-2021)

To understand the impact of the halving events, we can look at historical price movements during past cycles. Let's break down how the halving events in 2012, 2016, and 2020 have influenced the market.

1. **2012 Halving**:

    - The first Bitcoin halving in 2012 reduced the block reward from 50 BTC to 25 BTC. Following the event, Bitcoin's price saw a dramatic increase, rising from around $10 in November 2012 to over $1,000 by late 2013. This sparked mainstream awareness and the beginning of Bitcoin's journey into the public spotlight.

2. **2016 Halving**:

    - The second halving in July 2016 reduced the block reward from 25 BTC to 12.5 BTC. Similar to the first halving, the post-halving period saw a slow accumulation of demand, and by 2017, Bitcoin's price exploded, reaching its all-time high of nearly $20,000 in December. This bull run was fueled by growing institutional interest, media hype, and the overall optimism around the Bitcoin network.

3. **2020 Halving**:

    - The third halving in May 2020 reduced the block reward from 12.5 BTC to 6.25 BTC. Following this halving, the market experienced a much more sustained bull run, which continued into 2021. Bitcoin's price soared from around $9,000 at the time of the halving to over $60,000 in April 2021. Institutional investors such as Tesla, MicroStrategy, and others began to add Bitcoin to their balance sheets, signaling a shift in market sentiment toward mainstream acceptance.

4. **2024 Halving:**

   - The fourth halving occurring on April 19, 2024, reducing the reward from 6.25 BTC to 3.25 BTC. The market remained quite volatile leading up to the US Presidential election; however the price of BTC increased by 9% in the two days post the election. In December 2024, BTC broke the $100,000 barrier for the first time.

These cycles clearly demonstrate the correlation between Bitcoin's halving events and major shifts in market sentiment. As Bitcoin's supply becomes more limited and demand increases, the market moves through periods of speculative bubbles followed by corrections. However, the long-term trend remains upward, with each cycle pushing Bitcoin to new all-time highs.

Typical Phases of the Bull Cycle

A critical aspect of the four-year cycle is the way money flows through the market during different stages. As market confidence builds during the bull phase, investors tend to move their capital from lower-risk assets (like Bitcoin) into more speculative, higher-risk assets (like altcoins). Understanding this flow of capital can help you anticipate trends and time your trades more effectively.

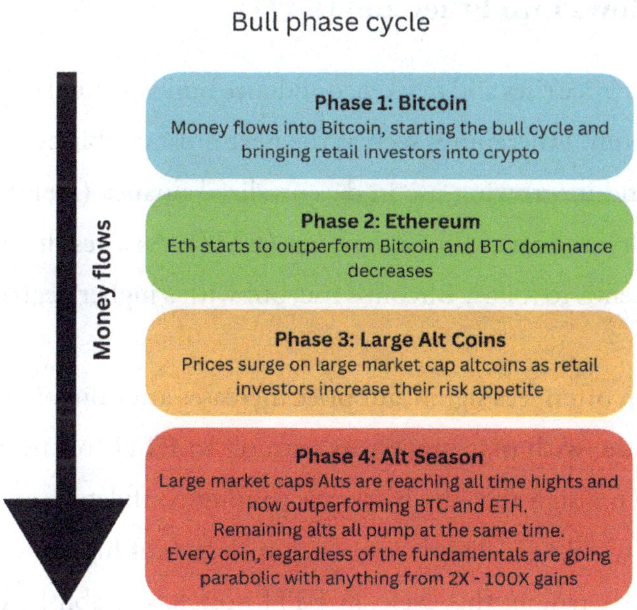

Money Flows into Bitcoin (BTC)

At the start of the bull cycle, Bitcoin remains the dominant asset in the market. As institutional interest rises and mainstream media covers Bitcoin's potential as a store of value, more investors pour money into Bitcoin. This is often referred to as a "flight to safety," as Bitcoin is perceived as the least risky cryptocurrency compared to others.

During this phase, Bitcoin's market dominance typically increases, and it sets the tone for the rest of the market. Traders and investors flock to Bitcoin as a way to participate in the bullish market without taking on the risks associated with smaller, less-established altcoins.

Money Flows into Ethereum (ETH)

As Bitcoin's price rises and market confidence builds, capital begins to flow into Ethereum. Ethereum is seen as the next most established blockchain network, and its growing use in decentralized finance (DeFi) and smart contracts drives demand for Ethereum (ETH). As a result, the price of Ethereum tends to follow Bitcoin's rise, but with a higher degree of volatility.

Ethereum often sees significant price increases after Bitcoin has entered its bull phase, with many investors turning to ETH for diversification. This is often a sign that the market is gaining confidence, and investors are willing to take on slightly more risk in search of higher returns. This is particularly true in this cycle, as ETH now has established Exchange Traded Funds (ETF) allowing greater exposure to the retail investor.

Money Flows into Large-Cap Altcoins

Once Bitcoin and Ethereum have surged, money begins to flow into larger-cap altcoins and 'Alt season' begins. These altcoins, which are typically well-established projects with medium market caps start to experience significant price increases as the broader market enters a more speculative phase.

At this stage, investors become more willing to take risks, and the market sentiment shifts toward higher returns. These altcoins are seen as having strong use cases, growing ecosystems, and increasing adoption, making them attractive investments.

Money Flows Down the Risk Curve (Smaller Altcoins and Memecoins)

As the bull market progresses and confidence continues to rise, capital flows further down the risk curve. Speculative assets like smaller altcoins and memecoins begin to experience rapid price increases. These assets often receive attention from retail traders and social media influencers, further fueling the speculative frenzy.

While these assets can see massive price increases, they are also highly volatile and risky. As a result, they often attract the most speculative capital during the final stages of a bull cycle. When the market becomes overheated, the bubble bursts, and these coins typically experience sharp declines in value.

Impact of the Four-Year Cycle on Major Cryptocurrencies and Market Sentiment

Understanding the four-year cycle and the flow of capital throughout the market is crucial for timing your investments. By recognizing the typical stages of a bull market and the role of Bitcoin's halving events, you can make more informed decisions about when to enter and exit positions in both major cryptocurrencies and altcoins.

The four-year cycle not only impacts Bitcoin and Ethereum, but also influences the broader market's sentiment, as investors move down the risk curve. When market confidence is high, altcoins rise in value, and speculative assets gain popularity. Conversely, during market corrections and bear phases, capital returns to Bitcoin as investors seek safety.

Timing Investments with the Four-Year Cycle

A prime example of successfully leveraging the four-year Bitcoin cycle comes from Michael Saylor, Executive Chairman of MicroStrategy, who has continued to strategically expand the company's Bitcoin holdings throughout 2024, aligning with his long-term investment thesis.

Between October 31 and November 10, 2024, MicroStrategy acquired approximately 27,200 Bitcoins, bringing their total holdings to 279,420 Bitcoins.

In December 2024, the company further increased its Bitcoin assets. Between December 2 and 31, MicroStrategy purchased an additional 45,370 Bitcoins, accounting for about 30% of all Bitcoin acquisitions made during that period.

By January 6, 2025, MicroStrategy's total Bitcoin holdings had reached approximately 447,470 Bitcoins, valued at over $45 billion, with an average purchase price of $62,473 per Bitcoin.

These strategic acquisitions underscore Saylor's unwavering confidence in Bitcoin's long-term value proposition and his commitment to leveraging market opportunities to strengthen MicroStrategy's position in the cryptocurrency market.

Using the Cycle to Inform Decision-Making

Understanding the phases of the cycle is key to making informed decisions. We explore the phases in more detail below.

The Accumulation Phase

This is the period following a market decline or after a bear market has ended or is ending. During accumulation, the market is generally quiet, with prices stabilizing at lower levels. Sentiment is often neutral or bearish, with many investors uncertain about the market's direction.

However, experienced traders recognize this phase as an opportunity. While others are sitting on the sidelines, those with a longer-term vision start buying. For crypto investors, this is where the potential for wealth begins to form. By entering early during the accumulation phase, you're positioning yourself to benefit from a future market rally.

In practice, the accumulation phase can be identified by relatively low trading volumes and sideways price action. If you're a long-term investor, this is an excellent time to start building positions in cryptocurrencies that you believe will perform well in the next cycle.

The Rally Phase (Bull Market)

Once the market breaks out of the accumulation phase, the rally phase begins. This is where prices start to rise, and positive sentiment begins to build. Investors who accumulated during the previous phase start seeing the benefits of their patience, and the buying pressure starts to drive prices higher. A rally is often triggered by a variety of factors—new market news, institutional adoption, or halving events in the case of Bitcoin.

During this phase, the crypto market often experiences strong upward momentum, leading to impressive gains. While the rally phase can be highly profitable, it's also critical to understand that this phase is often accompanied by a growing sense of euphoria. This is when market FOMO (fear of missing out) can cause prices to rise too quickly and lead to unsustainable bubbles.

As a trader, this is the phase where your profits can begin to snowball. However, it's important to keep a cool head and be ready to lock in profits when prices start to look overextended.

The Distribution Phase (Late Bull Market)

The distribution phase is the period during a bull market when prices begin to slow down. Investors who accumulated earlier in the cycle start to take profits, and the market begins to plateau. It can also be a time of high volatility as traders attempt to take advantage of short-term fluctuations. While some investors sell off their positions, others continue to buy, hoping for more gains.

For many traders, this is a time of cautious optimism. The smart money is selling into strength, while new buyers may be getting caught up in the excitement. Recognizing the distribution phase is essential in making the right decisions. If you're holding onto profits, this is a time to scale out of positions gradually and consider risk management strategies like stop losses or trailing stops.

The Decline Phase (Bear Market)

The bear market marks the end of the cycle, as prices begin to fall and sentiment shifts from bullish to bearish. This phase can feel like a long, drawn-out process, but it's also a time for savvy traders to reposition themselves for the next cycle. While many retail investors panic and sell at a loss, experienced traders know this is an opportunity to accumulate assets at a discount.

The decline phase can be brutal, but it's also where the most significant wealth-building opportunities lie. Those who understand market cycles and use this time to accumulate can be in a prime position when the next bull market begins.

The BTC Rainbow Chart: A Guide to the Market Cycle

To visually represent the different phases of the market cycle, we can look at the BTC Rainbow Chart. This chart uses a color-coded scale to indicate where Bitcoin's price stands in relation to past cycles.

The chart originated in 2014 from a Bitcoin Talk Forum user named Trololo. The chart is constructed using historical closing prices, then applying logarithmic regression to plot the data. The colored bands represent price change percentages. This makes it much simpler to comprehend the long-term trends and identify buying and selling opportunities.

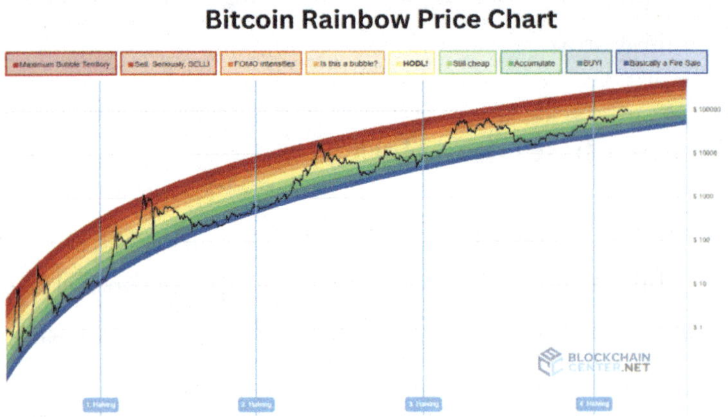

The colors range in nine shades from purple / blue to a dark red and the legends are seen in the image. A general description of the zones follows:

- **Red Zone**: Overbought. This typically happens when Bitcoin's price is nearing the top of a bull market. It's a warning that the market may be overheated and could be due for a correction.

- **Yellow to Green Zones**: Accumulation zones. These are periods when Bitcoin is trading at lower levels, often after a bear market, and prices are considered undervalued. These are the times when smart investors begin to buy, positioning themselves for the next rally.

- **Blue Zone**: Bear market lows. This is when prices are significantly lower, and it's often considered the best time to accumulate for long-term holders.

By using the BTC Rainbow chart as a guide, you can visually track the price levels and make informed decisions based on where the market is within the cycle. A word of warning though, the Rainbow Chart is not investment advice. Past performance is not necessarily an indication of future results – DYOR!

Spotting Trends and Aligning with Cycle Stages

Timing is everything in crypto trading, and aligning your trades with the natural cycle of the market can make all the difference. For example, Bitcoin's halving events—which occur every four years—are often followed by significant bull runs. These events, which reduce the supply of new Bitcoin entering the market, create scarcity and can trigger a surge in demand. Understanding these cycles and recognizing the right time to buy can give you a competitive edge.

Additionally, it's important to pay attention to overall market sentiment, news, and technical indicators. By combining your knowledge of the cycle with tools like moving averages, RSI, and support/resistance levels, you can increase the likelihood of successful trades.

Limitations of Relying Solely on the Four-Year Cycle

While understanding market cycles, particularly the four-year cycle, is an invaluable tool for crypto traders and investors, it is crucial to recognize that cycles are not foolproof. They provide a historical framework, but they don't guarantee future performance. Relying exclusively on the four-year cycle can be dangerous if it's treated as the only factor guiding your trading and investment decisions. The crypto market is influenced by numerous variables, many of which are unpredictable and not tied to the cycle. In this section, we will explore the limitations of relying solely on the four-year cycle, the external factors that can influence it, and how you can develop a more well-rounded strategy to better manage risk and maximize opportunities.

Cycles Aren't Guarantees: They're One of Many Factors

Cycles in any market—whether in traditional stocks, commodities, or cryptocurrencies—are based on historical trends. The four-year cycle in crypto, particularly for Bitcoin, has often shown a recurring pattern of accumulation, rally, distribution, and decline. But as any experienced trader will tell you, history does not always repeat itself in the exact same way.

The market cycles we observe are based on past data, and while they can offer valuable insights, they cannot predict the future with certainty. Factors that influenced past cycles may not apply in the same way in the future. For instance, a halving event may have triggered a price increase in previous cycles, but that doesn't guarantee it will have the same effect in subsequent halvings.

As much as we love the idea of a cyclical pattern, relying on it exclusively can lead to significant missteps, especially if the market deviates from the expected path. For example, if the cycle suggests that we're entering a bull market, but unforeseen events, like a global recession or government regulations intervene, the expected bullish behavior may not materialize. In these cases, the cycle may be delayed, altered, or entirely disrupted.

Thus, it's important to treat market cycles as guidelines, not absolutes. They can help you understand the general market trends, but they shouldn't be the sole determining factor in your decision-making process.

Macroeconomic Factors: Interest Rates, Regulations, Elections, and Their Impact on the Cycle

One of the key limitations of the four-year cycle is the external factors that can significantly impact the cryptocurrency market, often in ways that cycles cannot predict. Let's explore a few of the most important macroeconomic variables that could derail or accelerate the typical cycle:

1. **Interest Rates and Inflation**: Traditional financial markets are highly sensitive to changes in interest rates. When central banks (like the U.S. Federal Reserve) increase interest rates, borrowing becomes more expensive, which can reduce the amount of money flowing into riskier assets like stocks and cryptocurrencies. Rising rates can lead to lower demand for speculative assets, dampening the enthusiasm that drives bull markets in crypto.

In contrast, when interest rates are lowered or remain low for extended periods, money tends to flow more freely into riskier investments, including cryptocurrencies, as investors search for higher yields. For instance, during the COVID-19 pandemic, central banks around the world slashed interest rates to stimulate economic activity, which led to increased demand for alternative investments like Bitcoin. As a result, Bitcoin and other cryptocurrencies saw significant price appreciation during this period, even though the cycle was not following its traditional timeline.

Thus, while the four-year cycle may suggest a certain direction, interest rate changes can significantly alter the trajectory of the market. Interest rate hikes could potentially shorten the length of the cycle, whereas rate cuts may lengthen it or trigger an unexpected bullish rally.

1. **Government Regulations and Policy Changes**: The cryptocurrency market is still relatively young, and governments around the world are continuously grappling with how to regulate digital assets. Regulatory decisions can have profound impacts on the market, either boosting or stifling growth.

For example, in 2017, China's decision to ban cryptocurrency exchanges and initial coin offerings (ICOs) led to a sharp drop in Bitcoin's price. Similarly, in 2021, when El Salvador adopted Bitcoin as legal tender, it sparked a surge in interest and adoption, pushing Bitcoin to new highs. These regulatory actions are not tied to the four-year cycle but have far-reaching consequences for the market.

Uncertainty in regulation is also a key factor. If countries like the United States or the European Union decide to impose more stringent regulations on cryptocurrency exchanges, wallets, or even ownership, it could create a negative sentiment in the market, disrupting the expected cycle. Conversely, regulatory clarity or favorable legislation can spur new adoption and potentially accelerate a bull market.

1. **Elections and Political Events**: Political stability and the outcome of elections can influence investor sentiment in the crypto space. For instance, during election years, market uncertainty often increases as investors speculate on the policies of the incoming government. The results of elections can also affect the regulatory landscape for cryptocurrencies.

A change in leadership or government policies may lead to a favorable or unfavorable environment for cryptocurrency development and adoption. For example, if a country elects a president who is a strong proponent of blockchain technology and cryptocurrency, the market might experience a surge in confidence, potentially accelerating the upward momentum of the cycle. We are seeing this right now with President Elect Donald Trump. Following the election in November 2024, the price of Bitcoin rose 9% in two days! However, if a new administration views crypto as a threat or seeks to impose harsh regulations, it could trigger a market downturn, regardless of the phase the cycle is in.

Politics can cause unexpected disruptions to the cycle, highlighting the importance of considering geopolitical events and the broader political environment when evaluating market conditions.

The Importance of a Balanced Approach: Combining Cycle Knowledge with Other Indicators

Given the unpredictable nature of external factors, it's critical to adopt a more balanced approach to crypto trading and investing. While the four-year cycle can provide a helpful framework, it should be used in conjunction with other indicators and strategies to form a well-rounded decision-making process. Here are some ways to combine cycle knowledge with other tools:

1. **Technical Analysis (TA)**: One of the most popular tools for crypto traders is technical analysis, which involves using past price data and trading volumes to predict future price movements. Common technical indicators include the Relative Strength In-

dex (RSI), Moving Averages, Bollinger Bands, and MACD. These indicators help traders gauge whether an asset is overbought or oversold, whether a trend is strengthening or weakening, and when a potential reversal might occur.

By combining technical analysis with an understanding of the market cycle, you can make more informed decisions about when to enter or exit the market. For example, during a bull market (the rally phase of the cycle), if technical indicators suggest that Bitcoin is overbought and due for a correction, it may be wise to wait before entering or to scale out of positions.

1. **Sentiment Analysis**: Sentiment analysis is another critical tool for understanding market behavior. By gauging how investors feel about the market—whether bullish, bearish, or neutral—you can anticipate potential shifts in market direction. Sentiment can be influenced by news, social media trends, and even the broader economic environment.

During periods of extreme greed (e.g., right before the peak of a bull market), sentiment analysis may help you identify the warning signs of an impending market correction. Similarly, during periods of fear or pessimism, sentiment analysis can help you spot buying opportunities during market bottoms.

1. **Fundamental Analysis**: Finally, understanding the fundamental factors that drive cryptocurrency prices is key. This includes staying informed about the technological advancements, adoption rates, network upgrades, and overall use cases of the cryptocurrencies you're invested in.

For example, Bitcoin's halving events may be predictable, but it's also important to track the long-term development of the Bitcoin network (e.g., the Lightning Network) and the broader adoption of Bitcoin as a store of value and medium of exchange. Fundamental analysis helps you understand the broader forces driving demand for a particular cryptocurrency.

Adaptive Strategies: Preparing for the Unexpected

A crucial aspect of navigating the crypto market is adaptability. Given how unpredictable the market can be, it's essential to have a flexible approach that allows you to respond to changing conditions.

For instance, if the market cycle shows signs of shifting but you notice that external factors, like new regulations or economic events, are influencing the market differently than expected, you should be ready to adjust your strategies. This could mean reducing your exposure, hedging your positions, or waiting for more clarity before making further investments. The key is to stay informed, adjust your strategy as needed, and never rely on any one model or theory without considering the broader picture.

In conclusion, while the four-year cycle is an essential part of any cryptocurrency trader's toolkit, it is not a magic formula for guaranteed profits. External factors like macroeconomic conditions, political events, and regulatory changes can disrupt even the most predictable cycles. Therefore, it's vital to take a holistic and flexible approach that combines cycle knowledge with other indicators, and always be ready to adapt when the market deviates from expectations. By doing so, you'll be better prepared to navigate the dynamic and unpredictable world of cryptocurrency.

By combining your knowledge of the market cycle with sound trading strategies, you can set yourself up for long-term success in the exciting world of crypto.

Stay tuned, and let's dive deeper into the practical strategies that will help you navigate this ever-evolving market.

Chapter Three

Mastering Technical Analysis for Informed Decision-Making

Let's talk about Willy Woo, a well-known figure in the crypto space who exemplifies how mastering technical analysis can lead to success. Woo, a data scientist by profession, began his journey into the world of cryptocurrency with a deep understanding of market cycles and data analytics. While many new traders struggle to navigate the complexities of the crypto market, Woo applied his technical analysis skills to great effect, turning his interest in Bitcoin into a successful career as a leading on-chain market analyst.

In the early days of his crypto journey, Woo faced similar challenges to many beginners: unclear entry and exit points, unpredictable price movements, and a market rife with volatility. However, Woo leveraged his background in data science to dive into the technical analysis of Bitcoin's price movements. He focused on understanding price action, key indicators like the Relative Strength Index (RSI), moving averages, and volume analysis — tools that helped him better predict the market's next move.

Instead of relying on speculation or emotion-driven decisions, Woo used historical data to identify trends and patterns. Over time, he honed his skills in reading charts, identifying overbought and oversold conditions, and using market cycles to time his trades. His success grew as he accurately predicted Bitcoin's major price movements by tracking market sentiment and applying sound technical analysis. Today, Woo is one of the most respected voices in the crypto community, sharing his insights on Bitcoin's price movements and market cycles with his global audience.

This story shows that anyone, regardless of background, can leverage technical analysis to improve their trading strategy and make informed decisions. Willy Woo's rise is a testament to the power of learning the fundamentals of technical analysis, combining data-driven insights with a disciplined approach to navigating the crypto market. Whether you're new to crypto or an experienced investor, technical analysis can help you make smarter, more confident trading decisions and avoid costly mistakes.

In this chapter, we'll break down the core components of technical analysis—from understanding price action and candlestick patterns to using indicators like RSI and moving averages. By the end, you'll be equipped with the tools you need to enhance your trading and investing strategies.

The Basics of Technical Analysis

Technical analysis is the study of past market data, primarily price and volume, to forecast future price movements. While it might sound complex, at its core, technical analysis is all about understanding market sentiment—the collective psychology of buyers and sellers. The patterns created by this market sentiment are visualized in price charts, giving traders valuable insights into where the market might be headed.

Here's the beauty of technical analysis: it works on any market—stocks, commodities, and especially cryptocurrencies. The price movements you see on a crypto chart are a direct reflection of market psychology. By recognizing these patterns and trends, you can make more informed predictions about future price action. Now let's explore the fundamental components of technical analysis that will serve as the backbone of your trading strategy.

Understanding Price Action

The heart of technical analysis is price action — the movement of an asset's price over time. When you look at a chart, you're essentially observing how an asset has been priced by buyers and sellers at various points. Price action gives traders insights into market trends, momentum, and reversals, and it is often used in combination with other indicators.

One of the simplest ways to interpret price action is by analyzing higher highs and higher lows (bullish trends) or lower highs and lower lows (bearish trends). This basic principle helps traders understand the overall direction of the market.

For example, if you're looking at a Bitcoin chart and you see a series of higher highs and higher lows, this typically indicates a bullish trend. On the flip side, if the price is making lower highs and lower lows, it suggests a bearish trend, where sellers have the upper hand.

Price action is critical because it is real-time. It tells you exactly how the market feels right now and gives you the foundation to start making decisions about when to enter or exit a trade.

Trend Lines: Support and Resistance

Before diving into candlestick patterns, it's important to understand trend lines, which are essential in identifying support and resistance levels.

- **Support** is a price level where buying interest is strong enough to prevent the price from falling further. It acts as a "floor" that prices bounce off.

- **Resistance** is a price level where selling interest is strong enough to prevent the price from rising further. It acts as a "ceiling" that prices struggle to break through.

Support and Resistance Levels

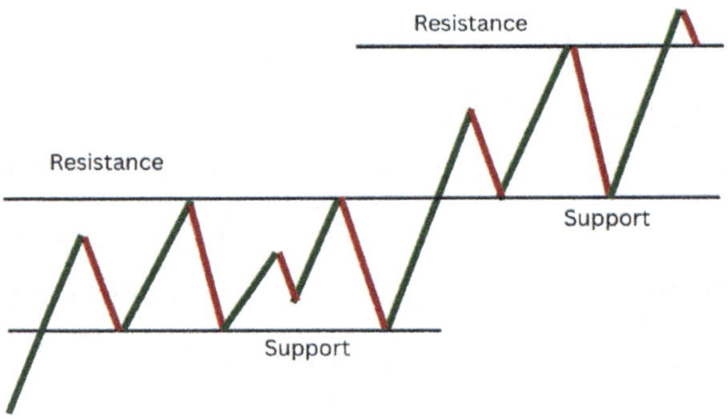

Trend lines connect significant highs or lows on a price chart, helping traders visualize these levels and anticipate potential price reversals. For example, if Bitcoin's price repeatedly bounces off $40,000, that level becomes a strong support. Conversely, if Bitcoin struggles to break above $45,000, that level becomes a key resistance.

By using support and resistance levels in conjunction with other tools, traders can better time their entries and exits.

Interpreting Charts for Better Decision-Making

One of the most powerful skills in a trader's toolkit is the ability to interpret charts accurately. Whether you're looking at a Bitcoin price chart or analyzing the movement of any cryptocurrency, charts are the visual representation of market sentiment. Mastering how to read charts, understand trends, and make predictions based on historical data is essential for making informed decisions and optimizing trading strategies. In this section, we will break down the essential concepts you need to know to read charts effectively, differentiate between trends and corrections, and use charts to confirm your trading decisions.

How to Read Charts: The Basics

At its core, reading a chart is about understanding price movement over time. Every point on a chart represents a price level at a specific moment, and when these points are connected over time, they form patterns and trends. By analyzing these patterns, traders can anticipate future price movement and make better decisions.

1. The Basics of a Price Chart: A price chart consists of several components:

- **Timeframe**: The horizontal axis of a chart represents time. It could be anything from minutes (for intraday traders) to years (for long-term investors). The choice of timeframe depends on your trading strategy.

- **Price Axis**: The vertical axis represents the asset's price, indicating how high or low the price has moved within a given time period.

- **Candlesticks**: These are the building blocks of charts. Each candlestick shows the open, high, low, and close prices for a specific time period. A green or white candle indicates a price increase, while a red or black candle represents a price decrease.

The shape, size, and color of these candlesticks can provide immediate insights into market sentiment. For example, a series of large green candles could indicate strong bullish momentum, while a series of red candles may suggest growing bearish pressure. These patterns are essential for interpreting chart data at a glance.

Candlestick Patterns: The Language of the Market

Now, let's take a deeper dive into one of the most popular tools in technical analysis: candlestick patterns. Candlesticks are a visual representation of price action over a specific time period. Each candlestick provides information about the open, close, high, and low prices within that time frame.

- **A bullish candlestick** (often green or white) indicates that the price closed higher than the opening price, suggesting buying pressure.

- **A bearish candlestick** (often red or black) shows that the price closed lower than it opened, suggesting selling pressure.

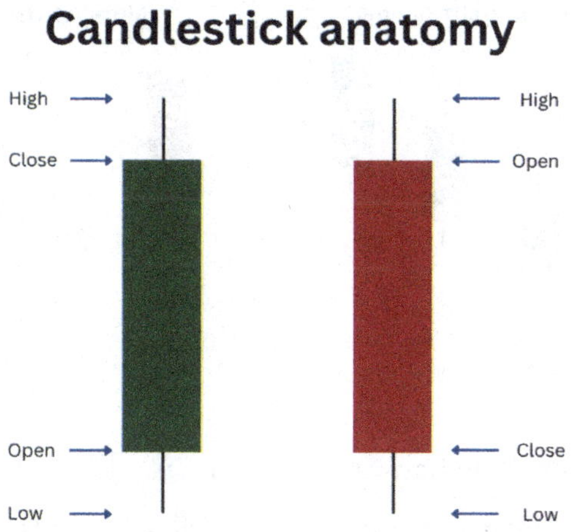

Candlestick patterns are key because they help traders identify potential market reversals or continuations. Let's examine some common patterns in greater detail.

Bullish patterns

Bullish patterns tend to occur after a downtrend and anticipate an upward reversal.

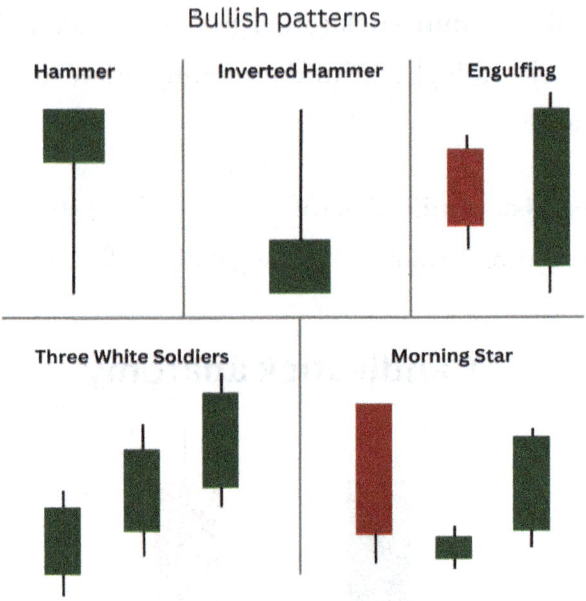

- **Hammer**: The hammer pattern has a long lower shadow, with a small body at the top of the candlestick with a small or non-existent top shadow. It appears in a downtrend and could signal a reversal to the upside. It suggests sellers are trying push the price down, but strong buying interest near the bottom recovers the session.

- **Inverted hammer**: Likewise, an inverted hammer indicates a potential price increase, or bullish reversal; however, the pattern looks opposite to the hammer. The small body will be at the bottom of the candle and the upper shadow will be twice as long as the body. This pattern indicates that buyers are trying to take control and push the price up.

- **Engulfing pattern (bullish)**: Indicates a potential reversal from a downtrend to an uptrend. After a red (or black) bearish candlestick, there is a larger green (or white) candlestick that engulfs the previous candlestick.

- **Morning star**: The morning star is a three-candle pattern. It consists of large bearish candle, a small indecisive candle (red or green) and a large bullish candle. This pattern indicates selling pressure is decreasing and buying pressure is increasing.

- **Three white soldiers**: This three-candle pattern shows a strong continuation of the bullish momentum. It consists of three consecutive bullish candles with higher closes, indicating upward momentum.

Bearish patterns

Bearish patterns are the opposite of bullish patterns and indicate a potential downtrend reversal.

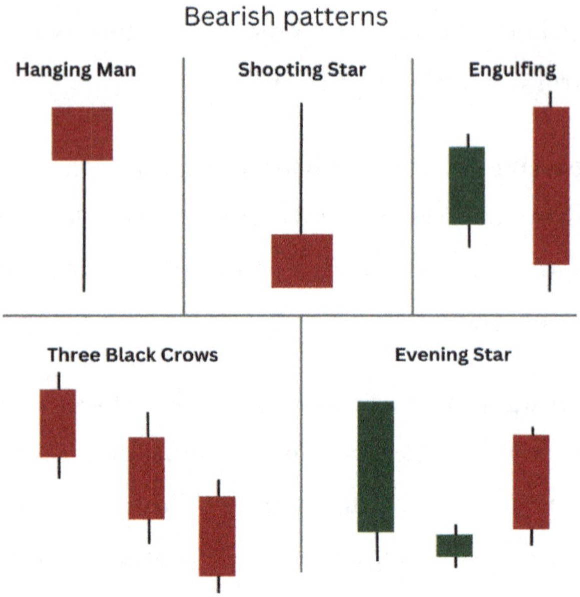

- **Hanging man**: The hanging man is the opposite of the hammer. It has a short body and a long lower shadow. The hanging man appears in an uptrend. There is selling pressure near the session's high, potentially signaling a bearish reversal.

- **Shooting star**: This is a bearish reversal pattern with a long upper shadow and a small body near the bottom. It suggests that sellers are gaining control or buyers have pushed prices higher but were overcome by sellers.

- **Engulfing pattern (bearish)**: Opposite to the bullish engulfing pattern, this pattern indicates a potential price drop. It is made up of two candles where a small bullish candle is followed by a large bearish candle that engulfs the previous bullish candle.

- **Evening star**: This is the bearish equivalent and opposite of the morning star pattern. It consists of a large bullish candle, a small indecisive candle and a large bearish candle.

- **Three black crows**: This pattern represents the opposite of the three white soldiers. In this pattern there are three consecutive bearish candles with lower closes, indicating a downward momentum.

Reversal or continuation patterns

Reversal and continuation patterns are used by traders to gauge momentum and trends in the market.

- **Doji**: This pattern indicates indecision in the market, where the opening and closing prices are almost the same. A Doji could signal that a trend is losing momentum and that a reversal may occur. Traders often look for confirmation in subsequent candles to act on a Doji signal.

- **Falling three methods**: This pattern consists of five candles and suggests a pause in the trend before its continuation. The falling three methods pattern is bearish. The first candle will be a large bearish candle and will be followed with three small bullish or stable candles. The fifth candle is a large bearish candle that should close below the first candle.

- **Rising three methods**: This pattern is the opposite of the falling three methods and indicates an upward continuation. The first candle is a large bullish candle that is followed by three, small bearish candles. The fifth candle is a large bullish candle that closes higher than the first candle.

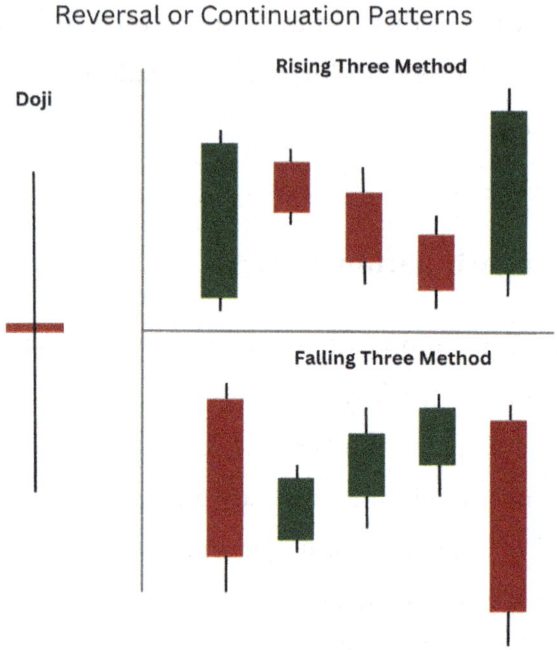

Price reversal patterns

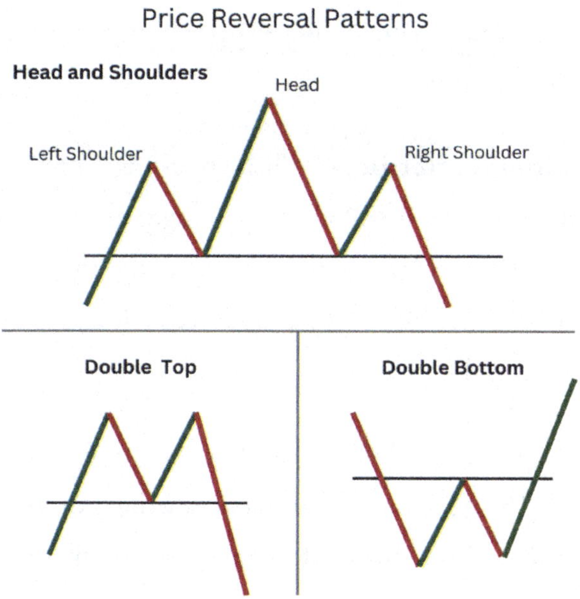

- **Head and shoulders**: This pattern is a reversal pattern indicating a trend change, often from bullish to bearish. It consists of three peaks: a higher peak (head) between two lower peaks (shoulders).
- **Double top**: A classic reversal pattern that signals a bearish reversal. This pattern occurs when the price hits a resistance level twice and fails to break through.
- **Double bottom**: The opposite of the double top, this pattern signals a bullish reversal that occurs when the price hits a support

level twice and bounces higher.

- **Hammer and Hanging Man**: Both patterns have long, lower shadows with small bodies at the top of the candlestick. A hammer appears in a downtrend and could signal a reversal to the upside, while a hanging man appears in an uptrend, potentially signaling a bearish reversal.

- **Engulfing Patterns**: A bullish engulfing pattern occurs when a small red candle is followed by a larger green candle, indicating a shift to buying pressure. A bearish engulfing happens when a green candle is followed by a larger red candle, signaling a potential bearish trend.

By recognizing these and other candlestick patterns, traders can anticipate possible price movements and make informed decisions. For beginners, understanding how these patterns form and what they represent is one of the most powerful tools in technical analysis.

Expanding Your Analysis with Indicators

Indicators provide additional layers of information to confirm trends or reversals and should also be used when trading to make informed decisions. In this section we will explore some of the more commonly used indicators.

RSI (Relative Strength Index)

The RSI is one of the most widely used momentum indicators in technical analysis. It measures the speed and change of price movements on a scale from 0 to 100, helping traders gauge whether an asset is overbought or oversold.

- An RSI above 70 typically indicates that an asset is overbought, suggesting that it may be due for a price correction or pullback.

- An RSI below 30 suggests that the asset is oversold, potentially indicating a buying opportunity if the market is about to reverse.

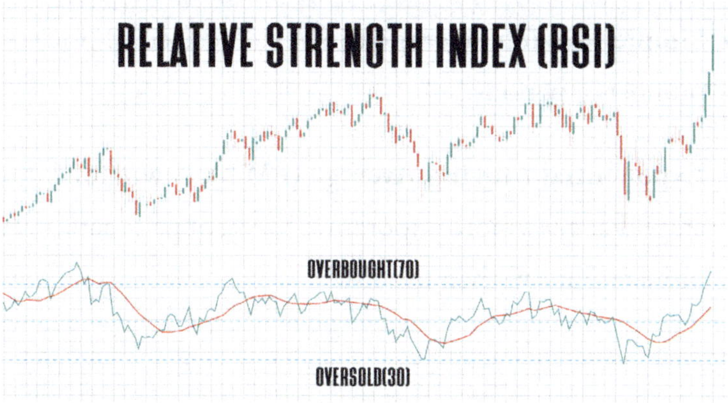

RSI is particularly helpful in range-bound markets, where the price tends to oscillate between overbought and oversold levels. On one hand, if Bitcoin's RSI hits 80 during a bullish rally, it might be an indicator that the asset is overextended and could experience a correction. On the other hand, if Bitcoin's RSI falls to 25 during a downtrend, it could signal a potential rebound or reversal in price.

For beginners, the RSI is an excellent starting point to gauge the strength of a trend and identify potential entry and exit points. It's not foolproof, but it offers valuable context for understanding market momentum.

Moving Averages: Smoothing Out the Noise

Another cornerstone of technical analysis is the Moving Average (MA), a tool that helps smooth out price data over a specified period. By calculating the average price over a set number of periods, moving averages help traders identify trends and potential support and resistance levels.

The two most commonly used moving averages are:

- **Simple Moving Average (SMA)**: The average price over a set number of periods.
- **Exponential Moving Average (EMA)**: A weighted moving average that gives more importance to recent price action, making it more responsive than the SMA.

A common strategy is to look for crossovers between short-term and long-term moving averages. For example, when the 50-day MA crosses above the 200-day MA, it's often seen as a bullish signal (a "Golden Cross"). Conversely, when the 50-day MA crosses below the 200-day MA, it can be a bearish signal (a "Death Cross").

Moving averages are useful in identifying the overall direction of the market. Whether you're looking at the long-term trend or short-term fluctuations, MAs help you visualize the market's underlying momentum.

MACD (Moving Average Convergence Divergence)

This indicator measures momentum by showing the relationship between two moving averages. When the MACD line crosses above the signal line, it's a bullish signal. When it crosses below, it's a bearish signal.

Bollinger Bands

These measure volatility. When prices move outside the bands, it often indicates overbought or oversold conditions, signaling potential reversals.

Why Basic Analysis Matters for Beginners

For beginners, mastering the basics of technical analysis is essential. Price action, candlestick patterns, RSI, and moving averages are not just theoretical concepts—they are practical tools that you can apply immediately to your crypto trading strategy. By understanding these elements, you'll be able to:

- **Identify trends** early, giving you an edge in timing your entries and exits.

- **Spot potential reversals** through candlestick patterns or RSI readings.
- **Manage risk** by understanding whether the market is overextended and adjusting your positions accordingly.

While there are more advanced techniques and indicators, these foundational tools will give you the confidence to start making informed decisions without being overwhelmed.

Practicing What You Learn

Theory alone isn't enough. Use demo accounts or small trades to practice applying these tools. Set clear entry and exit points, use stop-losses, and review your trades to refine your strategy. As you grow more confident, integrate more complex tools and indicators into your analysis.

Mastering technical analysis is a journey, but with discipline and practice, your trading performance and confidence in the crypto market can be significantly enhanced.

Fundamental Analysis: The Other Side of the Coin

While technical analysis focuses on price action and market sentiment, fundamental analysis delves into the intrinsic value of an asset, offering a more comprehensive understanding of its potential. In the world of cryptocurrencies, fundamental analysis involves evaluating the underlying factors that drive value and adoption.

Project Analysis

At the core of any cryptocurrency's value is its underlying technology, team, and use case. Evaluating the purpose of the project, its problem-solving capacity, and the expertise of the team provides insights into its long-term viability. For example, projects with innovative solutions, strong leadership, and clear roadmaps are more likely to succeed in gaining market adoption.

Adoption Metrics

The success of a cryptocurrency often hinges on its level of adoption. Analyzing wallet growth, transaction volumes, and active addresses provides a clear picture of the project's real-world utility and user base. For instance, a consistent increase in wallet growth suggests rising interest and trust in the project, which could translate to higher market value over time.

Market Sentiment

External factors, such as news, regulatory updates, and macroeconomic trends, play a significant role in shaping the market's perception of a cryptocurrency. Positive news, like partnerships or technological breakthroughs, can drive demand, while adverse events, such as bans or hacks, can lead to sell-offs. Staying informed about the broader market landscape ensures that traders and investors are prepared for potential price shifts.

Combining fundamental and technical analysis allows traders to adopt a holistic approach to decision-making. While technical analysis provides insights into price trends and market sentiment, fundamental analysis uncovers the long-term potential and sustainability of a project. Together, these methods empower traders to make more informed and confident decisions in the volatile crypto market.

Essential Tools and Resources

To effectively apply technical analysis and make informed decisions, it's crucial to have access to the right tools and resources. While understanding the core principles of technical analysis is essential, using the proper platforms, charting software, and data sources will ensure that you can apply these principles in real-time, accurately, and efficiently. Whether you're just starting out or are looking to level up your trading strategy, having the right tools will make your trading experience smoother, faster, and more profitable.

In this section, we'll explore the essential tools you need to carry out technical analysis, including trading platforms, charting software, and data sources. By the end of this section, you'll have a solid understanding of which resources are most reliable and how to leverage them to enhance your trading decisions.

Trading Platforms for Technical Analysis

A trading platform is your gateway to the market. It's where you place trades, track performance, and analyze price action. To effectively use technical analysis, you need a platform that provides the necessary charting tools, order execution features, and reliable access to market data. When choosing a trading platform, look for one that offers an intuitive interface, fast order execution, and comprehensive charting capabilities.

Here are some of the most popular and reliable trading platforms used by traders for crypto technical analysis:

1. **Binance**

    - **Overview**: Binance is one of the largest and most popular cryptocurrency exchanges in the world. It offers a wide range of digital assets, fast execution times, and an intuitive platform for trading.

    - **Why it's Great for Technical Analysis**: Binance provides advanced charting tools directly on the platform, including customizable charts, various time frames, and a wide range of technical indicators. You can easily apply RSI, moving averages, Bollinger Bands, and more while tracking real-time price action.

    - **Pros**: High liquidity, advanced charting features, access to over

200 cryptocurrencies.

- **Cons**: Complex for beginners, sometimes high fees depending on the trade volume.

2. **Coinbase Pro**

- **Overview**: Coinbase Pro (formerly GDAX) is an advanced version of the well-known Coinbase platform. It caters to traders who require more tools for detailed analysis.

- **Why it's Great for Technical Analysis**: Coinbase Pro offers a sophisticated charting interface, which includes several drawing tools, technical indicators, and customizable charting options. It also integrates well with trading algorithms, allowing for more professional-level analysis.

- **Pros**: User-friendly for advanced traders, integrates with a robust set of charts and tools, no withdrawal fees for certain cryptocurrencies.

- **Cons**: Not as many cryptocurrencies as Binance, higher fees than other platforms.

3. **Kraken**

- **Overview**: Kraken is another reputable cryptocurrency exchange with a strong emphasis on security and reliability. It provides users with access to a wide variety of coins.

- **Why it's Great for Technical Analysis**: Kraken offers advanced charting tools, real-time market data, and integration with third-party charting software like **TradingView**. Kraken's trading platform allows for detailed technical analysis through various indicators, patterns, and volume analysis.

- **Pros**: Excellent security features, highly rated for customer support, wide selection of cryptocurrencies.

- **Cons**: Can be a little overwhelming for beginners, higher fees for some transactions.

4. **eToro**

   - **Overview**: eToro is a social trading platform that allows users to trade cryptocurrencies and other assets. It's particularly known for its beginner-friendly interface and social trading features.

   - **Why it's Great for Technical Analysis**: eToro includes basic charting tools, such as indicators and chart patterns that help traders follow trends. While not as advanced as some other platforms, it's a great starting point for beginners who are still learning technical analysis.

   - **Pros**: Easy to use, good for beginners, social trading features.

   - **Cons**: Limited advanced charting tools, spreads can be high on some cryptocurrencies.

5. **Bybit**

- **Overview**: Bybit is a crypto derivatives platform that has grown rapidly due to its advanced features and user-friendly interface. It's designed for active traders looking for high leverage.
- **Why it's Great for Technical Analysis**: Bybit offers advanced charting tools, real-time price tracking, and integration with **TradingView** for detailed technical analysis. Bybit is well-suited for those who want to leverage their positions and apply advanced strategies.
- **Pros**: Low fees, highly advanced charting and analysis tools, leverage options.
- **Cons**: High leverage is risky, may not be suitable for beginners.

Charting Software for In-Depth Analysis

While trading platforms provide basic charting tools, charting software takes your technical analysis to the next level by offering more advanced and customizable features. Charting software is essential for traders who want to dive deep into price action, analyze multiple timeframes, and apply a range of technical indicators with greater precision.

Here are the top charting software options used by professional crypto traders:

1. **TradingView**

- **Overview**: TradingView is one of the most popular and powerful charting platforms in the world, used by traders across all markets—not just crypto. It's known for its sleek interface and vast library of technical indicators and charting tools.

- **Why it's Great for Technical Analysis**: TradingView allows you to customize your charts with a wide variety of indicators (RSI, MACD, moving averages, Fibonacci retracements, etc.), draw trendlines, and even use social trading features to see what other traders are analyzing. It also allows you to save your chart setups and share them with others.
- **Pros**: User-friendly, extremely customizable, integrates with most crypto exchanges, real-time updates.
- **Cons**: Some advanced features are locked behind a paid plan.

2. **CryptoCompare**

- **Overview**: CryptoCompare is a comprehensive crypto data provider that offers a charting platform along with real-time market data and portfolio management tools.
- **Why it's Great for Technical Analysis**: CryptoCompare provides access to historical data, real-time charting, and numerous indicators that can help you analyze market trends. It also offers a feature for comparing various assets across multiple exchanges.
- **Pros**: Detailed data analysis tools, multiple timeframes, broad selection of cryptocurrencies.

   - **Cons**: Less intuitive for beginners, interface is more cluttered than TradingView.

3. **MetaTrader 4/5 (MT4/5)**

   - **Overview**: Originally designed for forex trading, MetaTrader 4 and 5 have gained popularity in the crypto market for their powerful charting and technical analysis tools.
   - **Why it's Great for Technical Analysis**: MT4 and MT5 offer highly customizable charts, automated trading features, and advanced technical indicators. They also allow for backtesting strategies, a useful feature for traders looking to test their trading ideas before going live.
   - **Pros**: Robust features, automated trading, backtesting capabilities.
   - **Cons**: The interface can be difficult for beginners, fewer cryptocurrencies supported than on platforms like TradingView.

Data Sources for Accurate Market Information

To make informed decisions, you need accurate, up-to-date market data. Inaccurate or outdated data can lead to poor trading choices, so it's essential to rely on reliable data sources. Here are a few trusted sources for real-time crypto data:

1. **CoinMarketCap**

- **Overview**: CoinMarketCap is one of the most widely used websites for real-time data on cryptocurrency prices, market capitalization, volume, and circulating supply.
- **Why it's Great for Data**: It's an excellent resource for quickly checking the overall market sentiment, tracking the performance of individual cryptocurrencies, and analyzing historical price data.
- **Pros**: Free access to comprehensive market data, up-to-date pricing, historical charts.
- **Cons**: Sometimes data can be delayed during periods of high market volatility.

2. **CoinGecko**

- **Overview**: CoinGecko is another popular source for crypto market data. It provides comprehensive information on cryptocurrencies, including price charts, trading volume, and community engagement metrics.
- **Why it's Great for Data**: CoinGecko offers a wider range of metrics than many competitors, including developer activity and community metrics, which can give insight into the health of a crypto project beyond just price.
- **Pros**: Extensive data, free access to in-depth analytics, includes non-price data like community activity.

- **Cons**: Can be overwhelming for beginners due to the large amount of information.

Understanding Trends vs. Corrections

One of the most crucial distinctions every trader needs to understand is the difference between trends and corrections. These two concepts will guide your decision-making, helping you decide when to enter or exit trades.

1. What is a Trend? A trend refers to the general direction in which an asset's price is moving over a prolonged period. There are three primary types of trends:

- **Uptrend (Bullish Trend)**: A consistent movement in price upward, marked by higher highs and higher lows. An uptrend indicates that buyers are in control, and prices are generally rising.

- **Downtrend (Bearish Trend)**: A consistent movement in price downward, characterized by lower highs and lower lows. A downtrend signals that sellers are in control, and prices are generally falling.

- **Sideways/Flat Trend**: This is a market where prices move within a range, showing little directional movement. It's often a phase of consolidation, where the market is unsure of which direction to take.

Identifying Trends: To identify trends, traders use various tools such as trendlines, moving averages, and support and resistance levels. The key to spotting a trend is to look for consistent price movements in one direction over time. For example, if Bitcoin has been making higher highs and higher lows for several weeks, it's likely in an uptrend.

2. What is a Correction? A correction refers to a temporary reversal in price within a larger trend. These pullbacks are normal and often serve as opportunities to buy in a bullish market or sell in a bearish one. Corrections usually occur after a strong price move, where the market takes a breather and retraces some of the recent gains or losses.

Bullish Corrections: In an uptrend, a correction happens when the price temporarily drops after reaching new highs. This is healthy for the market because it helps prevent the asset from becoming overbought. If the correction is shallow, it can indicate that the uptrend is still intact, and the price will soon resume its upward momentum.

Bearish Corrections: In a downtrend, a correction may occur when the price temporarily rises after making lower lows. These short-term rises often trap unsuspecting buyers, but once the correction is over, the downtrend typically resumes.

How to Spot Corrections

- **Look for Short-Term Reversals**: Corrections usually involve quick price reversals that do not last long, unlike trends that persist over a more extended period.

- **Retracement Levels**: Many traders use Fibonacci retracements to identify the potential depth of corrections. If the price retraces to certain key Fibonacci levels (such as 38.2%, 50%, or 61.8%), it could be an indication that the correction is nearing its end.

Understanding whether the market is in a trend or a correction is vital because it helps you make better predictions about the future direction of price movement. If the market is in an uptrend and you see a correction, it may be a good opportunity to buy, as the overall trend is likely to continue. Conversely, if the market is in a downtrend and you see a correction, it may be a time to sell before the trend resumes downward.

Using Charts to Confirm Trading Decisions

Charts are not just for spotting trends or corrections—they are also used to confirm your trading decisions. Whether you're executing a short-term trade or long-term investment strategy, confirming your trade with chart data is important to ensure you are not making impulsive decisions.

Here's how to use charts to confirm your trading decisions:

1. Confirmation with Multiple Indicators: Traders often use multiple indicators to confirm their trades. For example, if you're considering a trade based on price action, you can confirm it by checking RSI levels or moving averages. If the price is in an uptrend, the RSI is above 50, and the price is above the 50-day moving average, that's generally a confirmation that the market is bullish.

Similarly, in a downtrend, if you see the price hitting resistance at a key level, while the RSI is above 70 (overbought), it may suggest that the price could soon reverse or experience a correction.

2. Candlestick Patterns for Confirmation: Certain candlestick patterns, like Doji, Engulfing, or Hammer patterns, can confirm a shift in market sentiment. For example, a bullish engulfing candle after a price pullback in an uptrend may signal a continuation of the bullish trend, confirming your buy decision. On the other hand, a bearish engulfing candle in a downtrend can provide confirmation to sell.

3. Volume as Confirmation: Volume is another essential element when interpreting charts. It provides information about the strength or weakness of a price move. A price move accompanied by high volume indicates strong conviction in that direction, while low volume suggests weak or unsustainable moves.

- **High Volume in a Trend**: If the price is trending upward with increasing volume, this confirms strong buying interest and the continuation of the trend.

- **Low Volume in a Correction**: If a price correction is accompanied by low volume, it suggests that the move may not be significant, and the trend may resume after the correction ends.

4. Support and Resistance Levels: Support and resistance levels act as psychological barriers in the market. If the price is approaching a support level in a downtrend and shows signs of a reversal, it can be a confirmation to buy, expecting the price to rebound. Similarly, if the price is approaching resistance in an uptrend and begins to show signs of stalling or reversing, it may be a confirmation to sell or short the asset.

Conclusion: The Art of Chart Interpretation

Interpreting charts is not just about reading price movements—it's about understanding the story behind the numbers and patterns. By differentiating between trends and corrections, and using charts to confirm your decisions, you'll be able to make more strategic, informed trades. Recognizing trends, understanding when they're likely to continue or reverse, and using tools like candlestick patterns, RSI, volume, and support/resistance levels to confirm your decisions will drastically improve your ability to navigate the crypto market.

As you become more familiar with reading charts and applying these techniques, you'll find that technical analysis becomes second nature. This will give you the confidence to make better trading decisions, avoid common mistakes, and ultimately, boost your profitability in the crypto space. Keep practicing, stay observant, and let the charts guide you toward smarter, more informed trades.

Chapter Four

Developing Your Personal Trading Strategy

JUST AS EVERY TRADER brings their unique perspective and goals to the crypto market, the strategy they choose should align with their individual circumstances, risk tolerance, and lifestyle. Let's explore the various trading approaches available and help you find the one that best suits your needs.

Understanding Different Types of Strategies

Imagine walking into a clothing store where every piece of clothing is labeled "one size fits all." While some items might work for you, others wouldn't provide the comfort or functionality you need. Trading strategies work the same way–what works perfectly for one trader might be completely unsuitable for another.

Let's break this down into four key strategies; scalping, day trading, swing trading and HODLing, to help you understand which might be the best fit for your personality and goals.

Scalping: The High-Speed Approach

Scalping in crypto trading is like being a convenience store owner who makes small profits on many transactions throughout the day. Instead of waiting for significant price movements, scalpers aim to profit from minimal price changes, often holding positions for just minutes or even seconds.

Pros:

- Potential for frequent small profits
- Reduced exposure to long-term market risks
- Less affected by major market trends
- Can be profitable in both bull and bear markets

Cons:

- Requires constant market monitoring
- High stress and intense focus needed
- Transaction fees can eat into profits
- Demands quick decision-making

- Needs sophisticated trading tools and platforms

Scalping might be right for you if you:

- Can dedicate full attention to trading
- Have a stable, high-speed internet connection
- Possess excellent emotional control
- Can make quick decisions under pressure
- Don't mind high-intensity activities

Day Trading: The Daily Grind

Day trading involves opening and closing positions within the same day, similar to running a food truck that starts fresh each morning and closes shop each night. Day traders typically analyze shorter timeframes and aim to profit from intraday price movements.

Pros:

- No overnight position risk
- Can capitalize on daily volatility
- Allows for regular analysis and planning
- Provides clear daily profit/loss metrics

Cons:

- Requires significant time commitment

- Can be emotionally draining
- Needs substantial market knowledge
- May miss longer-term trends
- Can lead to overtrading

Day trading could suit you if you:

- Have time to dedicate during market hours
- Enjoy technical analysis
- Can maintain emotional discipline
- Have a structured approach to trading
- Don't mind regular screen time

Swing Trading: The Middle Ground

Swing trading is like tending to a small garden. You plant seeds (investments) and nurture them over several days and weeks, as you wait for them to grow and yield a harvest (profit). Just as a gardener monitors the weather and adjusts their care routine, a swing trader keeps an eye on market trends and makes strategic decisions to maximize their returns. This strategy attempts to profit from 'swings' in price momentum, making it a perfect middle ground between day trading and long-term investing.

Pros:

- More flexible time commitment

- Lower stress than day trading
- Can capture larger price movements
- Allows for thorough analysis
- Better work-life balance

Cons:

- Overnight and weekend risk exposure
- Requires patience during consolidation periods
- May miss short-term opportunities
- Need for strong trend identification skills

Swing trading might be your style if you:

- Have a full-time job but want to trade actively
- Can handle holding positions during volatility
- Enjoy analyzing multiple timeframes
- Have patience to wait for setups
- Want to balance trading with other activities

HODLing: The Long-Term Vision

HODLing (an intentional misspelling of "holding" as this acronym means 'Hold on for Dear Life' in the crypto community) is like owning real estate – you're in it for the long haul, with your focus on value appreciation over time rather than short-term price fluctuations.

Pros:

- Minimal time commitment
- Reduced stress from daily fluctuations
- Lower transaction fees
- Can benefit from long-term crypto growth
- Easier to maintain regular employment

Cons:

- Requires strong conviction during downturns
- May miss trading opportunities
- Ties up capital for extended periods
- Need for extensive fundamental research
- Can be psychologically challenging during bear markets

HODLing could be perfect if you:

- Believe in the long-term potential of crypto

- Prefer a "set and forget" approach
- Have patience and strong conviction
- Don't need immediate access to invested capital
- Want to minimize time spent on trading

Creating a Strategy Based on Your Goals and Lifestyle

The most successful crypto traders aren't necessarily those with the most complex strategies or the most sophisticated tools–they're the ones whose trading approach aligns perfectly with their lifestyle, goals, and personal circumstances.

The crypto market has shown us time and again that success isn't about copying others' strategies– it's about finding what works for you. Take Michael Saylor, for instance. While his "never sell Bitcoin" approach worked brilliantly for MicroStrategy, converting nearly $4 billion of the company's treasury into BTC, this strategy wouldn't suit a day trader looking for regular income.

Setting Realistic Goals and Aligning Strategies

Let's look at how different successful traders have aligned their strategies with their goals.

Brian Armstrong, Coinbase's CEO, has consistently advocated for a long-term investment approach, focusing on fundamental value rather than short-term price movements. This strategy aligned perfectly with his goal of building a sustainable crypto business while maintaining his focus on running a major exchange.

In contrast, Sam Bankman-Fried (before FTX's collapse) made his initial fortune through arbitrage trading–spotting price differences between Asian and American crypto markets. This strategy required intense focus, sophisticated tools, and round-the-clock monitoring–clearly not suitable for someone with a full-time job outside crypto.

When setting your trading goals, consider these market-tested factors.

Time Commitment Reality Check

- How many hours can you realistically dedicate to trading?
- What times of day are you most alert and available?
- Do you have flexibility in your schedule?

Financial Objectives in Context

Consider the following questions and explore the approaches:

- Are you looking for primary income or supplementary earnings?
- What percentage return would satisfy your goals?
- How much capital can you comfortably risk?

If your intention is for the trading to become your primary income, then consider the following:

- Requires more active trading approaches
- Typically needs larger capital allocation
- Demands significant time investment
- Best suited for day trading or scalping
- Needs robust risk management

If your intention from trading is to supplement an existing income, combining spot trading with a crypto passive stream such as yield farming (more on this topic in future chapters) might be best. Consider the following:

- More flexible with capital requirements
- Allows for part-time commitment
- Can combine multiple strategies
- Lower pressure on consistent returns

If you are planning a longer-term investment, concentrate on accumulation through strategic DCA:

- Favor HODLing with strategic positions
- Focus on fundamental analysis
- Less time-intensive

- Can start with smaller capital
- Emphasis on project research (fundamental analysis) and market cycles

The 2022 bear market particularly highlighted how different strategies performed under stress. While many day traders struggled with decreased volatility, those who had diversified into staking and yield farming maintained more stable returns.

Benefits of Personalized Strategy Development

Real market events have demonstrated these key advantages in having a personalized strategy:

1. **Improved Consistency**

The May 2021 crash showed why personalized risk management matters. Traders who had developed strategies aligned with their risk tolerance were more likely to survive the 50% BTC drop, while those copying others' strategies often panic-sold at the bottom. By having your own established strategy, you will benefit from the following advantages:

- Better adherence to trading rules
- More systematic approach to market analysis
- Clearer entry and exit criteria
- Reduced emotional decision-making
- Enhanced performance tracking

2. Better Work-Life Balance

During the DeFi summer of 2020, many traders learned this lesson the hard way. Those who tried to catch every yield farming opportunity burned out quickly, while traders with clear strategies and boundaries maintained sustainable profits. Again, by sticking with your personal strategy, you'll have:

- Reduced stress from forcing unsuitable strategies
- More sustainable long-term approach
- Better integration with existing commitments
- Improved focus during trading sessions
- Higher quality of life

3. Enhanced Decision Making

Look at the NFT boom of 2021. Traders who stuck to their strategies (whether focusing on art NFTs, gaming tokens, or metaverse assets) generally outperformed those who chased every trending project. Highlights:

- Clearer framework for market analysis
- More confident trading decisions
- Better risk management
- Improved position sizing
- More systematic profit-taking

4. Increased Profitability Potential

James, a teacher, developed a strategy combining swing trading during school terms with more active trading during holidays. His personalized approach included:

- Morning analysis before school (30 minutes)
- Position checks during lunch break
- Detailed weekend planning sessions
- More active trading during school holidays
- Focus on 4-hour and daily timeframes

This strategy works because it:

- Fits his available time
- Matches his risk tolerance
- Aligns with his schedule
- Leverages his analytical skills
- Provides sustainable results

Process to Develop Personalized Strategy Development

The process of developing your personalized strategy should include:

1. **Self-Assessment**

- Evaluate your trading knowledge
- Assess your technical capabilities
- Consider your risk tolerance
- Review your available resources
- Analyze your personality traits

2. Goal Setting

- Define clear financial objectives
- Set realistic time commitments
- Establish risk parameters
- Create measurable milestones
- Plan for strategy evolution

3. Strategy Testing

- Start with paper trading
- Test different timeframes
- Evaluate various indicators
- Track results systematically
- Adjust based on performance

4. Implementation

- Begin with smaller positions
- Gradually increase exposure
- Monitor strategy effectiveness
- Make data-driven adjustments
- Keep detailed trading logs

Remember, your strategy should evolve as your circumstances change. Regular review and adjustment of your approach ensures it continues to serve your goals effectively while maintaining alignment with your lifestyle and resources.

A well-aligned strategy becomes your personal roadmap to success in the crypto markets, providing clarity in decision-making and confidence in execution. Take the time to develop yours thoughtfully – it's an investment that will pay dividends throughout your trading journey.

Backtesting and Adjusting Your Strategy

Success in crypto trading isn't about finding the perfect strategy immediately–it's about continuous refinement and adaptation. Just as a chef perfects a recipe through multiple iterations, your trading strategy should evolve through careful testing and adjustment. Thus, the crypto market's rapid evolution demands constant strategy refinement. The transition from the 2021 bull market to the 2022 bear market provided a master class in strategy adaptation.

Understanding Backtesting

Backtesting is like having a trading time machine–it allows you to test your strategy against historical data before risking real capital. Here's how to approach it effectively:

1. **Data Collection**

- Gather historical price data
- Include volume information
- Consider market conditions
- Note significant events
- Document social media trends

2. Testing Parameters

- Define clear entry/exit rules
- Set specific time periods
- Include transaction costs
- Account for slippage
- Consider market liquidity

3. Results Analysis

- Calculate win/loss ratios
- Measure profit factors
- Evaluate drawdowns
- Assess risk metrics
- Track consistency

Remember, the crypto market's dynamic nature means no strategy stays perfect forever. The key is to build a flexible approach that can evolve with the market while you stay true to your personal goals and risk tolerance.

As Changpeng Zhao (CZ) often says, "Protect your investments first, profits come second." This principle has proven especially valuable during major market transitions and should be a cornerstone of any trading strategy.

Measuring Success and Making Adjustments

To determine if your trading strategy is meeting your trading goals, you need to be able to measure success. Below you will find useful information on how to measure your strategy.

1. **Quantitative Metrics:**

- Win rate percentage
- Average profit per trade
- Maximum drawdown
- Risk-adjusted returns
- Sharpe ratio

2. Qualitative Factors:

- Emotional stability
- Strategy adherence
- Decision confidence
- Time management
- Overall satisfaction

Remember that strategy adjustment is an ongoing process, not a one-time event. The crypto market's dynamic nature requires traders to remain flexible and adaptive. Your strategy should be robust enough to handle various market conditions while being flexible enough to evolve with changing circumstances.

Success comes not from finding a perfect strategy, but from developing one that you can execute consistently and adjust as needed. Keep testing, keep learning, and most importantly, keep adapting to the ever-changing crypto landscape.

Chapter Five

Building a Balanced Crypto Portfolio with Strategic Asset Allocation

PICTURE TWO CRYPTO INVESTORS during the tumultuous market of 2022: Alex and Maria. Alex had gone all-in on Terra LUNA, attracted by its promising yields and apparent stability. Maria, meanwhile, had built a diversified portfolio spanning Bitcoin, Ethereum, select DeFi tokens, and some exposure to NFT gaming projects. When LUNA collapsed in May 2022, Alex lost nearly everything, while Maria's balanced approach meant she maintained most of her capital despite the broader market downturn.

This real-world example from 2022 perfectly illustrates why understanding crypto categories and building a balanced portfolio isn't just about maximizing gains–it's about surviving the inevitable market cycles that define crypto investing.

Crypto Categories and Narratives

Before diving into specific categories, let's understand what is meant by "narratives" in crypto. Think of narratives as compelling stories that drive investor interest and market momentum. The NFT boom of 2021 wasn't just about digital art–it was about the narrative of digital ownership and exclusive communities. Similarly, the AI narrative of 2023 and now the AI Agent narrative in late 2024 wasn't just about artificial intelligence–it was about the future of autonomous systems and decentralized intelligence.

Narratives can shift rapidly. Remember how quickly the "DeFi Summer" of 2020 transformed into the "NFT Spring" of 2021? Or how the "Metaverse" narrative of late 2021 gave way to the "Meme" narrative of 2024? Understanding these shifts is crucial for portfolio management.

Whilst there are no 'official' cryptocurrency categories and different websites will have slight variances, there are common categories across the crypto communities. We will explore the main ones below.

Layer 1 Coins (L1s)

Layer 1 blockchains are the backbone of the crypto ecosystem, providing the fundamental infrastructure upon which other projects are built. Think of them as the internet protocols of the crypto world.

Major Layer 1 Platforms and Their Value Propositions

Bitcoin (BTC)

- The original cryptocurrency
- Primarily regarded as digital gold and a store of value
- Demonstrated resilience through multiple market cycles
- Increasing institutional adoption (Tesla, MicroStrategy, nation-states)

Ethereum (ETH)

- The leading smart contract platform
- Successful transition to Proof of Stake in 2022
- Ethereum Virtual Machine (EVM) compatibility
- Strong developer community and network effects

Solana (SOL)

- Known for high speed and low transaction costs
- High scalability and high transaction throughput
- Growing retail adoption through Solana Mobile
- Strong presence producing MEMEs

Other Notable L1s

- Cardano (ADA): Academic approach to blockchain development
- Avalanche (AVAX): Subnet technology for customized blockchains
- Sui (SUI): A newer blockchain with a focus on scalability and performance

Why L1s Matter for Your Portfolio

Layer 1s typically offer several key benefits:

- Greater stability during market downturns
- Strong network effects and established communities
- Clear technological value propositions
- Institutional investment support

Consider how Ethereum maintained significant value through the 2022 bear market, while many smaller projects disappeared entirely.

This resilience is why many investors use L1s as their portfolio foundation.

DeFi Coins: The Future of Finance

Decentralized Finance (DeFi) represents a paradigm shift in how we think about financial services, leveraging blockchain technology to conduct financial transactions without the need for traditional intermediaries like banks or brokers. From lending platforms to decentralized exchanges, DeFi is reimagining traditional financial systems.

In this section, we are focusing on DeFi as a category of Cryptocurrency. However, if you would like to learn and understand more about DeFi, refer to ***Crypto Essentials Book Two*** where I have dedicated a chapter to deep dive into this topic.

Leading DeFi Protocols

- **Aave: P**ioneer in flash loans and multi-token lending. Allows users to lend crypto assets and borrow against them as collateral, earning interest on deposits.
- **Uniswap:** A leading decentralized exchange (DEX) that facilitates efficient peer-to-peer token swaps
- **MakerDAO:** A decentralized stablecoin (DAI)
- **Lido:** Allows users to stake their ETH and receive a liquid token (stETH) that can be used in other protocols

Evaluating DeFi Projects

- Check Total Value Locked (TVL) trends
- Assess revenue generation mechanisms
- Review smart contract audits

- Monitor developer activity
- Evaluate governance structures

Meme Coins

Meme coins represent the intersection of social media, community engagement, and cryptocurrency. While often dismissed as purely speculative, they've demonstrated remarkable staying power and occasional profound impact on the broader market.

Notable Meme Coin Phenomena

Dogecoin (DOGE)

- Started as a joke in 2013
- Gained mainstream attention through Elon Musk's endorsements
- Demonstrated surprising longevity and use cases
- Peaked at $88 billion market cap in 2021 and now sits around $57 billion market cap (early 2025)

Shiba Inu (SHIB)

- Built a comprehensive ecosystem from a meme beginning
- Developed Shibarium Layer 2 solution
- Expanded into DeFi and NFTs

- Showed how meme coins can evolve

Pepe (PEPE)

- Pepe the Frog is a cartoon character that was created in 2005
- Became a meme token in the cryptoverse in April 2023 as a symbol of rebellion, decentralization and community
- Explosive growth upon launch and experienced a meteoric rise

Risk Management for Meme Coins

Meme coins are extremely volatile and have seen significant gains and significant losses. Due to the speculative nature of these tokens, they are deemed high risk. To minimize your risk with memes, follow the below guidance:

- Limit exposure to 1-5% of portfolio
- Use strict stop-loss orders
- Monitor social media sentiment
- Watch for celebrity involvement
- Track community growth metrics
- Research the developers and review the whitepaper

Cautionary Tale

The Squid Game Coin (SQUID) of October 2021 served as a warning about meme coin risks. SQUID was inspired by the hugely popular Netflix series, *Squid Game*, though there was no affiliation with Netflix or the *Squid Game* creators.

The creators of SQUID created the hype needed for a successful launch. The coin rose 83,000% in a week with retail investors buying at all price levels due to FOMO.

On November 1, 2021, the anonymous creators of SQUID executed a 'rug pull'. In short, the creators sold all their holdings and disappeared. When the creators dumped their tokens, the liquidity was drained, rendering the token worthless and the price fell significantly.

At the same time, investors were unable to sell their tokens due to the restrictions that were coded into the tokens smart contract. Investors were left with tokens that were not worth anything.

There were some red flags with SQUID from the beginning that were ignored:

- Whitepaper–poorly written with grammatical errors throughout
- Project's website and social media accounts –no transparency about the developers

This is a real life scenario on a meme coin, but the lessons are relevant for all cryptocurrencies.

AI and AI Agents: The Next Frontier

The AI narrative exploded in 2023, driven by advances in large language models and autonomous systems. This category represents the intersection of blockchain technology with artificial intelligence to create innovative solutions in areas such as data sharing, automation and decentralized decision making.

Key Players in the AI Crypto Space

Artificial Superintelligence Alliance (FET)

- A merger between Fetch (FET), Ocean (OEAN) and SingularityNET (AGIX)
- Created a unified, decentralized AI ecosystem
- Pioneered autonomous AI agents for DeFi
- Created marketplace for AI data trading

Render (RENDER)

- Provider of decentralized GPU based rendering solutions
- A platform for artists and developers to build services and applications with high levels of scale, speed and efficiency

Bittensor (TAO)

- An open-source protocol that powers a decentralized, blockchain based machine learning network

- Utilizes a distributed ledger for the development and distribution of artificial intelligence technology

Virtuals Protocol (VIRTUAL)

- Blockchain-based system to create digital worlds or economies where people, businesses and AI systems can interact
- Allows developers to build virtual spaces (like metaverses), games or applications where assets and services are managed through blockchain

Gaming and GameFi

The gaming sector represents one of crypto's most promising mass adoption vectors, combining entertainment with economic incentives. It introduces play-to-earn (P2E) mechanics, asset ownership and decentralized economies to traditional gaming.

Major Gaming Ecosystems and GameFi tokens

ImmutableX (IMX)

- Layer 2 solution on Ethereum
- Partnerships with major game publishers
- Zero gas fees for players
- Strong focus on traditional gaming integration

GALA Games (GALA)

- Multiple game ecosystem approach across genres such as RPGs and simulations
- Built sustainable revenue model for players

Beam (BEAM)

- BEAM token is the native asset for the BEAM gaming network, powered by the Beam DAO
- Flexible software development kit that enables game developers to choose from a variety of tools

Real World Assets (RWA)

RWAs represent the convergence of traditional finance with blockchain technology, offering a new way to invest in physical assets through tokenization. In simple terms, it is bringing tangible real-world items like real estate, stocks, bonds, or commodities onto the blockchain.

The RWA's are tokenized, meaning they are converted into digital tokens that represent ownership or a share of an asset.

Leading RWA Protocols

MakerDAO (DAI)

- Tokenizeddebt and stablecoins
- Uses real-world assets like loans or bonds as collateral to issue its

decentralized stablecoin (DAI)

Centrifuge (CFG)

- Specialized in tokenizing real-world invoices
- Supply chain finance solutions
- SME financing opportunities
- Institutional adoption focus

Goldfinch Protocol (GFI)

- Crypto-backed real-world lending
- Focus on emerging markets
- Uncollateralized lending structure
- Demonstrated sustainable yield generation

The success of RWA integration in protocols like MakerDAO has shown that traditional finance and crypto can coexist effectively, providing stability during market volatility while maintaining the benefits of blockchain technology.

Remember, each of these categories plays a specific role in a well-balanced crypto portfolio. The key is to understand how these narratives evolve and interact, allowing you to adjust your allocation strategy accordingly. The next section will explore how to determine the right mix of these assets for your specific goals and risk tolerance.

Market Caps and Defining the Risk Profile of a Coin or Token

A cryptocurrency's market capitalization—calculated by multiplying the total circulating supply by its current price—is an important metric to evaluate its risk profile. Market cap helps investors gauge the relative size, stability, and maturity of a crypto asset.

- **High Market Cap (> $10 billion)**: Coins with high market caps, such as Bitcoin and Ethereum, are well-established and have a proven track record. These assets are generally considered lower risk, as they tend to be more resilient during market downturns. While they may not offer astronomical gains, they provide a degree of stability and security in a volatile market.

- **Medium Market Cap ($1 billion – $10 billion)**: These are projects that have shown significant growth potential but are less established than high-cap coins. Examples include Mantra (OM) and Uniswap (UNI). While medium-cap coins carry more risk than high-cap assets, they can provide higher returns if their ecosystems continue to grow.

- **Low Market Cap (< $1 billion)**: Low-cap coins are typically new or niche projects with limited adoption and liquidity. They offer the potential for outsized gains but come with the highest risk. Many low-cap tokens fail to gain traction and disappear, making due diligence critical when considering investments in this category.

Aligning Market Cap with Risk Profiles

Understanding the relationship between market cap and risk can help you decide how much of your portfolio to allocate to each category. For example:

- **High-Cap Coins**: Ideal for investors seeking long-term stability and lower volatility.
- **Medium-Cap Coins**: Suitable for moderate risk-takers aiming for steady growth.
- **Low-Cap Coins**: Best for experienced investors willing to accept high volatility and potential losses in exchange for high rewards.

Portfolio Structure: Setting Up for Low, Medium, and High Risk

Building a balanced portfolio requires aligning your asset allocation with your risk tolerance, investment goals, and market understanding. Below, we outline three portfolio structures for low, medium, and high-risk strategies.

Low-Risk Portfolio Allocation

A low-risk portfolio prioritizes stability and capital preservation. This approach suits conservative investors or those new to the crypto space.

Suggested Allocation:

- 60% High market cap coins and stablecoins such as Bitcoin (BTC) and Ethereum (ETH). These assets provide a strong foundation of stability. Bitcoin and Ethereum are resilient during market downturns, while stablecoins offer a safe haven during periods of extreme volatility.

- 30% Medium market capaltcoins: Allocate this portion to well-established Layer 1 or DeFi projects with proven use cases.

- 10% High-Risk altcoins that have a lower market cap. For potential high returns, include a small percentage of emerging narratives or speculative projects, like AI tokens or new gaming tokens.

Why It Works: This structure allows you to participate in crypto growth while minimizing the risks of significant losses. For example, during the 2022 bear market, portfolios heavily weighted in Bitcoin and Ethereum outperformed those reliant on speculative low-cap coins.

Medium-Risk Portfolio Allocation

A medium-risk portfolio balances growth potential with stability, making it suitable for investors willing to accept moderate volatility for higher returns.

Suggested Allocation:

- 30% High market cap coins and stablecoins. This foundational allocation ensures your portfolio has a stable core to weather market downturns.

- 60% Medium market capaltcoins. Focus on established projects and spread this allocation across multiple narratives, such as DeFi, Layer 1 blockchains, RWA and gaming ecosystems.

- 10% High-Risk altcoins that have a lower market cap. Include emerging narratives or high-potential projects but limit individual exposure to avoid overconcentration.

Key Strategies for Medium-Risk Portfolios:

- Diversify within categories: For example, split your medium-risk allocation between Layer 1 coins and top DeFi protocols.

- Avoid allocating more than 20% of your portfolio to a single narrative to mitigate sector-specific risks.

- Monitor market sentiment and rebalance quarterly to maintain your desired risk profile.

Why It Works: Medium-risk portfolios offer a blend of stability and growth, allowing you to capture opportunities in emerging sectors without exposing yourself to excessive volatility. For instance, investors with medium-risk portfolios during the 2020-2021 bull run benefited from both Bitcoin's stability and the explosive growth of DeFi projects.

High-Risk Portfolio Allocation

A high-risk portfolio focuses on maximizing growth, making it suitable for experienced traders who can tolerate significant volatility.

Suggested Allocation:

- 30% High market cap coins and stablecoins. A minimal allocation here provides a safety net while keeping the focus on higher-risk assets.

- 40% Medium market capaltcoins. Include strong performers with growth potential across narratives you feel will perform the most strongly this cycle.

- 30% High-Risk altcoins with low market caps. Allocate speculative projects in trending narratives like AI tokens, meme coins, or new GameFi projects. Ensure these assets are spread across multiple categories to mitigate sector-specific risks.

Key Strategies for High-Risk Portfolios

- Set strict stop-loss orders to limit potential losses on speculative trades.

- Regularly evaluate projects for updates on development, partnerships, and market trends.

- Be prepared for emotional highs and lows due to significant price swings.

Cautionary Note: High-risk strategies often underperform in bear markets. For example, during the 2022 crypto winter, portfolios heavily weighted in high-risk altcoins suffered devastating losses. Historical data shows that low and medium-risk strategies tend to deliver more consistent returns over multiple market cycles.

Finding Your Balance

Building a balanced crypto portfolio requires understanding your risk tolerance and aligning it with a strategic allocation plan. Whether you're prioritizing stability, growth, or aggressive gains, a well-structured portfolio will ensure you are prepared to navigate the market's ups and downs.

Remember, diversification is your ally. By spreading your investments across high, medium, and low-risk assets, as well as different narratives, you reduce the risk of catastrophic losses while maintaining exposure to crypto's immense growth potential. As you continue to learn and adapt, evaluate and rebalance your portfolio regularly to align with your goals and the ever-evolving market landscape.

Adapting and Rebalancing Your Portfolio

As with any investment strategy, adapting and rebalancing your portfolio is crucial to maintaining a healthy, risk-adjusted investment plan. The cryptocurrency market is dynamic and unpredictable, and staying nimble is key to successfully navigating both bullish and bearish cycles. In this section, we'll explore the importance of periodic rebalancing, adapting to market shifts, and taking advantage of new trends—all while keeping your portfolio in line with your evolving financial goals.

Periodic Rebalancing and Risk Adjustment

One of the most important aspects of managing a crypto portfolio is periodic rebalancing. This means reviewing your portfolio's performance and adjusting the allocation of your assets to ensure they remain aligned with your risk tolerance and investment objectives. Here's why it's important.

Why Rebalancing is Crucial:

- **Market Shifts**: Cryptocurrencies can experience massive fluctuations in value, causing your portfolio's risk profile to shift dramatically. For example, if a particular altcoin surges in value, it may start to make up a larger portion of your portfolio than you initially intended, increasing your exposure to that asset.

- **Emerging Trends**: As new narratives and technologies emerge, your portfolio might need to adjust to reflect these changes. If a promising new DeFi protocol, NFT gaming platform, or Layer 1 blockchain arises, you'll want to consider how it fits within your existing strategy.

- **Changing Goals**: Your financial goals may evolve over time. As you move closer to your objectives, such as retirement or a major purchase, you may decide to lower your risk exposure and shift towards more stable assets like Bitcoin, Ethereum, or stablecoins.

Tips for Adjusting Allocations

- Regularly Review Performance: Depending on the risk allocation of your strategy, I would recommend reviewing your strategy every 2-5 months, revisit your portfolio to check the performance of individual assets. If one asset has appreciated significantly, consider rebalancing to lock in profits and bring the allocation back in line with your goals.

- Adjust Based on Market Conditions: If you anticipate a market downturn (e.g., based on historical cycles), increase your allocation to low-risk assets like Bitcoin or stablecoins to protect your capital. Conversely, when entering a bull market, consider adding more exposure to higher-risk assets for growth potential.

- Gradual Risk Reduction: As your portfolio grows and you accumulate more capital, consider gradually reducing your exposure to high-risk assets. For example, after a successful bull market, move some of your profits into more stable assets to protect against future downturns.

David, an investor who entered the market during the 2017 bull run, buying a variety of altcoins with high potential. By 2018, when the market tanked, he realized his portfolio had become heavily concentrated in small-cap coins that had lost significant value. By the time the market recovered in 2021, David had learned his lesson. He began rebalancing his portfolio more frequently, selling off high-risk assets at the peak of the market and moving profits into Bitcoin and Ethereum. This shift allowed him to preserve much of his capital during the 2022 bear market, while still having exposure to emerging trends.

Market Timing and Recognizing Portfolio Shifts with the Four-Year Cycle

The cryptocurrency market is notorious for its volatility, and understanding market cycles is one of the most important tools for rebalancing your portfolio. As we've seen in previous chapters, the four-year cycle (largely driven by Bitcoin's halving events) can have a significant impact on the market's risk profile.

How Portfolio Risk Changes Throughout the Cycle

- **Bull Markets**: In a bull market, risk tends to increase as investors chase higher returns. During these periods, portfolios with a higher allocation to medium and high-risk assets (such as DeFi coins, meme coins, and emerging narratives) are likely to see substantial growth. However, this comes with increased volatility.
- **Bear Markets**: Conversely, bear markets are characterized by

widespread declines, and portfolios with high-risk exposure can suffer substantial losses. This is a time to reduce exposure to volatile assets and increase allocation to low-risk assets like Bitcoin, Ethereum, or stablecoins.

Rebalancing Before a Predicted Bear Market

If market signals or cycle analysis suggests a coming bear market (such as when the halving effect starts to lose its momentum), consider increasing your allocation to low-risk assets:

- Shift funds into Bitcoin, Ethereum or Solana, which tend to be more resilient during downturns.
- Consider adding stablecoins to preserve capital in case of further declines.
- If your portfolio is heavily weighted toward DeFi or meme coins, it may be wise to reduce exposure to these areas, as they are more vulnerable to market downturns.

Re-entering High-Risk Assets During Bull Markets

When the market enters a new bull phase, high-risk assets — especially those in emerging narratives like AI, Gaming, and RWA—tend to offer greater potential for growth. During these periods, you can:

- Gradually increase your exposure to emerging sectors but do so with discipline and risk management in mind. Avoid going all-in on any one narrative.

- Take profits as prices rise, and gradually allocate those profits back into core assets like Bitcoin and Ethereum.

Practical Advice for Taking Profits and Reinvesting

- During market highs, sell a portion of your high-risk assets to lock in profits and protect gains.
- Reinvest those profits into core assets such as Bitcoin and Ethereum, which provide long-term stability.
- Rebalance by reallocating funds across both low and medium-risk assets, maintaining a diversified approach to avoid putting all your eggs in one basket.

Evaluating New Trends and Adapting to Market Shifts

Crypto markets are driven by narratives, and as we've seen, these narratives can shift rapidly. To stay ahead of the curve, it's essential to evaluate new trends carefully before incorporating them into your portfolio.

Tips on Evaluating New Coin Narratives

- **Research the Technology**: Before diving into a new trend, make sure you understand the technology behind it. Is the project solving a real-world problem? Does it have a clear value proposition, or is it just hype?

- **Look for Long-Term Potential**: Not every new narrative will stand the test of time. While it's tempting to chase the latest trend, focus on assets that have real utility and long-term growth potential. Avoid jumping on trends just because they're popular at the moment.

- **Evaluate the Team**: A strong development team is critical to a project's success. Check the team's background, expertise, and previous projects to assess their credibility and ability to execute the vision.

Guidance on Risk of Chasing Trends

While it's important to be open to new trends, it's equally important to avoid chasing short-lived narratives. Many projects that seem promising in the short term fail to gain traction or disappear entirely. Before jumping into a new trend, ask yourself:

- Does this project align with my portfolio's goals and risk tolerance?

- Am I willing to commit long-term, or is this just a speculative investment?

Checklist for Assessing New Coins

- **Utility**: Does the coin solve a real problem, or is it purely speculative?
- **Community**: Is there an active, engaged community behind the project?
- **Partnerships**: Are there strong, credible partnerships supporting the project?
- **Market Position**: Where does the coin rank in terms of market cap and adoption?
- **Development Activity**: Is the project actively being developed, and are there frequent updates?

Chapter Six

Advanced Strategies for Earning Passive Income in Crypto

Consider Lena, a crypto investor who, like many others, started with a simple buy-and-hold strategy. She had a share of Bitcoin and Ethereum in her portfolio and was primarily focused on price appreciation. But in 2020, she discovered the world of staking and yield farming. Eager to grow her assets without having to trade actively, Lena decided to explore these passive income strategies.

By staking some of her Ethereum and participating in yield farming on a decentralized finance (DeFi) platform, Lena was able to earn consistent returns on her holdings. Over the next few months, she saw her portfolio grow at a rate far beyond what she would have earned through price appreciation alone. By the end of the year, Lena had generated double-digit returns on her staked assets and additional rewards from yield farming—all while holding her investments long-term.

Lena's story highlights the power of passive income in the crypto world. By strategically leveraging staking, yield farming, and liquidity provision, she was able to enhance her portfolio's value without needing to constantly monitor the market. In this chapter, we'll dive into these strategies and show you how they can help you grow your crypto wealth.

Introduction to Passive Income in Crypto

Passive income refers to earning money without actively engaging in the day-to-day management of an asset. In the world of traditional finance, this might look like earning interest from a savings account or collecting rent from a property. In the crypto space, passive income comes in several forms; including staking, yield farming, and liquidity provision.

The Different Passive Income Streams, Benefits and Risks

Below we will explore each of the three passive income streams mentioned above, how they work and their benefits and risks.

Staking

Staking is generally the simplest and least risky form of passive income in crypto. It's a great entry point for beginners who are just starting to explore passive income strategies.

By locking up your crypto on a Proof of Stake (PoS) blockchain, validators are chosen to create new blocks and validate transactions based on the amount of cryptocurrency they have staked. The more you stake, the higher your chances of being chosen to validate transactions and earn rewards. The rewards are often a portion of the new coins generated by the blockchain. Think of staking as earning interest on a fixed deposit.

Staking is straightforward to set-up and possible on common networks and through exchanges.

The rewards for staking vary depending on the platform and blockchain. For example, ETH 2.0 offers yields of around 4 – 6% per annum whilst Cardano offers 4-5% depending on the pool you choose.

The benefits to staking include:

- **Relatively Low Effort**: Compared to yield farming, staking is simpler and requires less active management.

- **Lower-Risk**: For well-established assets like Ethereum or Cardano, staking is relatively low-risk compared to other strategies such as trading.

- **Security**: Staking is usually done directly on the blockchain, meaning the security of the network is tied to your staking activity.

- **Compounding Rewards**: Some platforms allow you to automatically reinvest your rewards, increasing your staking balance over time.

Risks include:

- **Lock-Up Periods**: Staking may involve a lock-up period, where you cannot access your staked assets for a set amount of time.

- **Slashing**: Some networks penalize stakers for malicious activity, which can lead to the loss of some of your staked assets.

- **Market Volatility**: While staking earns rewards, the value of the staked cryptocurrency can decrease if the market price drops, reducing the real-world value of your holdings and rewards.

- **Technical or Platform Risk**: If the staking platform or network you're using experiences a hack, bug, or failure, your staked funds could be at risk.

Yield Farming

Yield farming involves providing liquidity to decentralized finance (DeFi) platforms in exchange for rewards. By supplying your crypto to a pool, you earn interest or tokens (not necessarily the same token you are farming), often at a higher rate than traditional savings accounts. In yield farming, it is common to move, or farm, your crypto to different pools or platforms to get the best return.

Yield farming is a bit more complex than staking and the Total Value Locked (TVL), Annual Percentage Yield (APY), and the reputation of the platform should be evaluated before participating.

The benefits of yield farming include:

- **High Returns**: Yield farming typically offers higher returns than staking, especially if you're willing to take on more risk.

- **Multiple Income Streams**: Farmers can earn rewards in the form of platform tokens, transaction fees, or interest, depending on the

DeFi protocol.

- **Flexibility**: Unlike staking, your assets can often be withdrawn more easily.

- **Compounding Opportunities**: Farmers can reinvest their rewards into the same or other liquidity pools, increasing their earning potential through compounding.

Key risks related to yield farming include:

- **Impermanent Loss**: If the price of the assets you provide changes significantly, you could end up with less value than you started with.

- **High Complexity:** Navigating DeFi platforms and understanding yield farming strategies can be complicated, especially for beginners. Mistakes in transactions or choices can lead to losses.

- **Rug Pulls:** Some yield farming protocols may be scams, where developers withdraw all the funds from the pool and disappear, leaving investors with nothing.

Liquidity Provision

This involves providing your crypto to a pool that helps others trade on the decentralized exchanges (DEXs). Think of this as providing money to a currency exchange booth so they can swap currencies for others. In return, you get a share of the trading fees.

As a liquidity provider, you supply equal amounts of two assets (e.g., ETH and USDT) to a pool. In return, you receive LP (Liquidity Provider) tokens, which represent your share in the pool and can be redeemed for the liquidity you've provided plus fees earned.

Key benefits to liquidity provision include:

- **Earn Passive Income**: LP's earn a share of the trading fees generated on DEXs like Uniswap or PancakeSwap.

- **Compounding Returns**: With staking and yield farming, rewards are often compounded, meaning you earn more rewards on your existing rewards, accelerating portfolio growth.

- **Portfolio Growth**: These strategies allow you to grow your crypto assets passively, providing a steady stream of income without the need for active trading.

- **No Lock-Up (in Some Pools):** In most cases, you can withdraw your liquidity at any time, offering flexibility compared to other forms of crypto passive income streams.

However, passive income strategies are not without risks. Some key risks include:

- **Impermanent Loss**: This occurs when the price of the assets in the liquidity pool changes, and you end up with a lower value than if you had just held the assets outside of the pool.

- **Market Volatility**: While you earn rewards, the value of your underlying assets can still fluctuate, especially in the crypto market.

- **Platform Risks**: DeFi platforms and staking services can face hacks, bugs, or mismanagement, which might lead to losses.

Who Should Consider Passive Income Strategies?

Passive income strategies are suitable for a variety of crypto investors, but they can be particularly beneficial for:

- **Long-term Investors**: Those who hold assets with a long-term perspective and are not actively trading may find staking and yield farming attractive.

- **Low-Trade Individuals**: If you don't have the time or inclination to actively monitor the market and trade frequently, passive income allows you to earn while you sleep.

- **Conservative Investors**: Even conservative investors can consider passive income strategies, but they should be cautious. For example, they may prefer staking Bitcoin or Ethereum, which are relatively lower-risk options compared to newer DeFi tokens.

Integrating Passive Income into Existing Portfolios

Once you've selected a strategy, you can gradually integrate passive income into your portfolio. For example, start by staking a portion of your crypto holdings to generate passive rewards while keeping the rest for long-term growth. Over time, you can increase the portion of your portfolio allocated to passive income-generating assets.

Chapter Seven

Risk Management and Protecting Your Investments

In early 2021, Tom, a novice crypto trader, spotted a promising altcoin project generating hype on social media. Driven by FOMO, he poured a significant portion of his portfolio into the coin without researching its fundamentals or setting safety nets like stop-loss orders. Initially, the price surged, but when the market corrected, the altcoin's value plummeted over 90%. Tom's lack of a risk management strategy turned what could have been a calculated investment into a devastating loss.

Tom's experience underscores the importance of risk management in crypto investing. Whether you're trading actively or holding long-term, protecting your investments is just as critical as growing them. In this chapter, we'll dive into practical strategies to calculate risk, diversify your portfolio, and avoid common pitfalls.

Calculating Risk and Reward

Every trade involves risk, but not all risks are created equal. Assessing the risk of a trade involves weighing its potential downside against its expected upside.

Key Steps to Assess Risk:

1. Research the Asset: Understand the coin or token you're trading. Check its market cap, liquidity, and use case.

2. Determine Volatility: Volatile assets are riskier. Use indicators like Bollinger Bands or average true range (ATR) to measure price fluctuations.

3. Risk-Reward Ratio: Calculate the ratio of potential profit to potential loss. To calculate the ratio, you need to estimate the profit you will make from the trade and divide this number with your initial investment. A common benchmark is a 2:1 ratio—your expected profit should be at least twice your potential loss. Whilst common, this is still quite high risk and a ratio of 4:1 is more conservative.

4. Position Sizing: Limit each trade to a small percentage of your total portfolio (e.g., 2-5%) to minimize exposure and only have a few trades open at a time.

Balancing Potential Gains and Losses

Risk management isn't about avoiding all risks—it's about taking calculated risks. Here's how to balance gains and losses effectively:

- **Set Clear Goals**: Decide your entry and exit points before initiating a trade. Don't let emotions dictate your decisions.

- **Accept Small Losses**: Small losses are a natural part of trading. The goal is to ensure your wins outweigh your losses over time.

Stop-Loss and Take-Profit Orders

Stop-loss and take-profit orders are essential tools for protecting your investments:

- **Stop-Loss Orders**: Automatically sell your asset when its price falls to a predetermined level. For example, if you buy Bitcoin at $30,000, setting a stop-loss at $28,000 ensures your maximum loss is $2,000.

- **Take-Profit Orders**: Automatically sell when the price reaches your target profit. For instance, if your target price is $35,000, a take-profit order locks in gains when Bitcoin hits that level.

Pro Tip: Use a trailing stop-loss to lock in profits while allowing for continued upside during price rallies. A trailing stop-loss automatically adjusts your stop-loss price based on the price movement. A trailing stop-loss can be a dollar amount or percentage from the current price. As the price increases, the trailing stop increases in line with the price movement.

Managing Portfolio Risk

Diversifying Assets

Diversification is one of the most effective ways to reduce portfolio risk. By spreading your investments across different assets and sectors, you minimize the impact of a single asset's poor performance.

How to Diversify Effectively:

- Include Different Crypto Categories: Allocate funds to Layer 1 and coins (e.g., Bitcoin, Ethereum), DeFi tokens, and emerging narratives like gaming or AI.

- Use Stablecoins for Stability: Stablecoins like USDT or DAI provide a hedge against volatility, allowing you to preserve capital during market downturns.

- Invest in tokens with different market caps. See previous chapters on portfolio allocation for examples.

Benefits of Diversification:

- Risk Reduction: Poor performance in one category can be offset by gains in another.

- Consistent Growth: A diversified portfolio captures opportunities across multiple sectors.

Hedging Strategies

Hedging involves taking offsetting positions to reduce the impact of market volatility and protect your investment against losses. Think of hedging as an insurance policy for your portfolio–while it doesn't eliminate risk entirely, it can help you minimize potential downsides.

Below are some popular hedging strategies that traders and investors use to hedge their positions:

- Short Selling: This involves borrowing an asset and selling it at its current price with the intention of buying it back later at a lower price. If the price of the asset drops, the profit from short selling can offset losses in other parts of your portfolio.

- Options Trading: Use options to hedge against price swings. Options give you the ability–but not the obligation–to buy or sell an asset at a predetermined price. For example, buying a *put option* allows you to sell an asset at a fixed price, protecting against downside risk if the market takes a downturn.

- Stablecoin Holdings: As stablecoins are pegged to stable assets, like fiat currencies, they can act as a buffer during market turbulence. Allocate a portion of your portfolio to stablecoins during uncertain market conditions to reduce exposure to volatility.

Benefits of Hedging:

- Risk Reduction: Hedging can help you cushion losses during sudden market downturns.

- Portfolio Stability: By diversifying risk, hedging strategies can provide a measure of stability in your investments.
- Flexibility: You can adjust your hedging approach based on market conditions, personal risk tolerance, and investment goals.

Risks and challenges of hedging

While hedging can be an effective strategy, it's not without its challenges:

- Cost: Hedging often involves additional fees, such as trading fees for options or short selling. These costs can eat into your profits.
- Complexity: Some hedging strategies, like options trading, can be technically complex and require a solid understanding before implementation.
- Missed Gains: By focusing on minimizing losses, you might limit your potential for larger profits during bull markets.

Stay Disciplined, Stay Informed

Risk management is the backbone of successful crypto investing. By calculating risks, diversifying your portfolio, and avoiding common pitfalls, you can protect your investments and navigate the market with confidence. Remember, the crypto market is volatile, but with the right strategies, you can turn risks into opportunities while preserving your capital for long-term growth.

Chapter Eight

Advanced Strategies for Experienced Traders

FOR THOSE WHO HAVE mastered the basics of cryptocurrency trading and are ready to dive deeper, advanced trading strategies provide opportunities to maximize gains and capitalize on market inefficiencies. However, these strategies require a disciplined approach, a strong understanding of the market, and effective risk management. In this chapter, we'll explore two key advanced trading strategies: margin trading and leverage, and arbitrage opportunities.

Margin Trading and Leverage

Margin trading allows traders to borrow funds to increase their trading position, thereby amplifying potential profits. However, the use of leverage also magnifies risks, making it a double-edged sword. While experienced traders can benefit from margin trading, it requires a sound strategy and strict risk controls.

Pros, Cons, and Best Practices for Margin Trading

Pros of Margin Trading:

- Amplified Returns: Margin trading increases your buying power, enabling you to profit more from smaller price movements.
- Flexibility: It allows traders to take advantage of both bullish and bearish markets by going long or short.
- Diversification: Leverage can free up capital, enabling traders to spread investments across multiple assets.

Cons of Margin Trading:

- Increased Risk: Losses are magnified, and without proper risk management, positions can be liquidated.
- Interest Costs: Borrowed funds come with interest, which can erode profits, especially if trades take longer than expected to play out.
- Complexity: Margin trading involves sophisticated strategies and is not suitable for beginners.

Best Practices:

1. Start with Low Leverage: Use minimal leverage (e.g., 2x or 3x)

when starting to minimize risks.

2. Set Stop-Losses: Protect yourself from significant losses by setting stop-loss orders to automatically close positions.

3. Monitor Market Trends: Margin trading requires close monitoring of market movements to avoid sudden liquidation.

4. Limit Position Size: Never risk more than 5% of your portfolio on a single trade, especially when leveraging.

Risks of High Leverage

Leverage can be both a blessing and a curse. High leverage ratios (e.g., 50x or 100x) might seem appealing, but they are extremely risky and can lead to rapid losses.

How High Leverage Works

If you use 10x leverage on a $1,000 position, you control $10,000 worth of assets. A 10% price increase results in a 100% gain ($1,000 profit), but a 10% price drop wipes out your entire investment.

Common Pitfalls:

1. Liquidation: If the price moves against your position beyond a certain threshold, your position will be liquidated, resulting in a total loss.

2. Market Volatility: Crypto markets are highly volatile, and even

small price swings can trigger liquidation on high-leverage trades.

3. Overconfidence: The potential for large gains can lead to reckless trading without proper analysis.

Setting Leverage Limits

To trade responsibly with leverage, setting strict limits is essential:

- Define Your Risk Tolerance: Only use leverage ratios that align with your ability to absorb potential losses.
- Use Risk Management Tools: Employ tools like stop-loss orders and trailing stops to protect your positions.
- Diversify Trades: Avoid putting all your leveraged trades into a single asset; diversify to spread risk.

Example: An experienced trader uses 3x leverage on Bitcoin and sets a stop-loss at 5% below the entry price. This way, even if the market moves against them, their losses are contained to 15% of their leveraged position.

Arbitrage Opportunities

Arbitrage involves exploiting price differences for the same asset across different markets or platforms. In the fast-paced and volatile crypto market, arbitrage can be highly profitable but requires quick execution and precision.

Identifying and Executing Profitable Arbitrage

Arbitrage is the simultaneous buying and selling of an asset to profit from price differences between exchanges. For example, if Bitcoin is trading at $30,000 on Exchange A and $30,200 on Exchange B, a trader can buy Bitcoin on Exchange A and sell it on Exchange B for a $200 profit per Bitcoin.

Steps to Identify Arbitrage Opportunities:

1. Monitor Prices: Use tools or platforms like CoinGecko, CryptoCompare, or specialized arbitrage bots to track price discrepancies.

2. Evaluate Fees: Account for transaction and withdrawal fees, which can eat into profits.

3. Ensure Liquidity: Confirm that the exchanges involved have sufficient liquidity to execute trades quickly.

Types of Arbitrage in Crypto

1. **Spatial Arbitrage**: This involves exploiting the price differences between two geographically different exchanges. Example: Buying Bitcoin in a market with lower demand (e.g., Exchange A) and selling it in a market with higher demand (e.g., Exchange B).

2. **Triangular Arbitrage**: This involves trading between three currency pairs within the same exchange. For instance, trading BTC/USDT → ETH/USDT → ETH/BTC to profit from small discrepancies.

3. **Cross-Exchange Arbitrage**: Buy an asset on one exchange where it is undervalued and sell it on another where it is overvalued.

4. **Statistical Arbitrage**: Use algorithms and historical data to identify and exploit statistical inefficiencies.

5. **DeFi Arbitrage:** DeFi platforms often have price discrepancies due to liquidity differences. Arbitrageurs can exploit these differences by swapping tokens on platforms like Uniswap, SushiSwap, or PancakeSwap.

Challenges of Arbitrage

1. Execution Time: Crypto markets move quickly, and opportunities can disappear within seconds.

2. Fees: High transaction and withdrawal fees can negate potential profits, especially for small-scale arbitrage.

3. Regulatory Risks: Some jurisdictions may impose restrictions on cross-border trading or arbitrage activities.

Example: A trader identifies a $50 price difference for Ethereum between two exchanges. After accounting for fees, they execute the trade and secure a $30 profit. However, if fees are overlooked, a trade could result in a net loss.

Advanced trading strategies like margin trading and arbitrage offer experienced traders significant opportunities to maximize profits. However, these strategies come with heightened risks and require a disciplined approach, effective risk management, and thorough market analysis. By starting small, using leverage responsibly, and continuously monitoring arbitrage opportunities, traders can enhance their profitability while mitigating potential losses. As with all crypto investments, staying informed and adaptable is crucial for long-term success in this dynamic market.

Algorithmic and Bot Trading

As cryptocurrency markets operate 24/7, human traders face limitations in constantly monitoring and acting on market movements. Algorithmic trading and trading bots offer a solution, allowing traders to automate their strategies, execute high-frequency trades, and capitalize on market inefficiencies with speed and precision. However, while automation can enhance profitability, it requires careful planning, reliable software, and robust risk management.

Using Automation to Enhance Profitability

Algorithmic trading involves using pre-programmed rules and strategies to execute trades automatically. These algorithms analyze market data, identify patterns, and make trades based on predefined conditions, all without human intervention.

Advantages of Algorithmic Trading

1. Speed and Efficiency: Bots can process vast amounts of data and execute trades faster than any human.

2. Emotion-Free Trading: Automated systems stick to strategies without being influenced by fear or greed.

3. Round-the-Clock Trading: Bots operate 24/7, ensuring no market opportunity is missed.

Common Types of Bots

- Market-Making Bots: These bots create buy and sell orders to profit from the spread between bid and ask prices.

- Arbitrage Bots: They monitor multiple exchanges to identify and exploit price discrepancies for the same asset.

- Trend-Following Bots: These bots use technical indicators to detect trends and execute trades accordingly.

Setting Up a Trading Bot

1. Choose a Reliable Platform: Popular platforms like 3Commas, Pionex, Bybit, or CryptoHopper provide user-friendly interfaces for setting up trading bots.

2. Define Your Strategy: Customize the bot to align with your goals, whether that's scalping, arbitrage, or trend-following.

3. Backtest the Bot: Before deploying it live, test the bot using historical market data to evaluate its performance.

4. Monitor Performance: While bots are autonomous, regular monitoring ensures they function as intended and adapt to changing market conditions.

Risks and Challenges of Algorithmic Trading

While trading bots can be profitable, they are not foolproof. Understanding their limitations and associated risks is crucial.

1. Over-Reliance on Automation: Bots operate based on their programming and cannot account for unexpected events like flash crashes or major news announcements.

2. Market Volatility: Sudden market movements can lead to significant losses if the bot is not programmed with risk management features.

3. Technical Issues: Bugs, internet connectivity problems, or exchange outages can disrupt bot operations.

4. Fees and Costs: High-frequency trades incur transaction fees, which can erode profits if not carefully managed.

Risk Mitigation Tips

- Use bots only as part of a diversified trading strategy.
- Set stop-loss and take-profit levels within the bot's parameters.
- Avoid deploying bots during highly volatile events like earnings announcements or regulatory changes.

Conclusion

Algorithmic and bot trading can transform how experienced traders engage with the crypto market by offering speed, efficiency, and scalability. However, success requires choosing reliable platforms, crafting robust strategies, and actively managing risks. By leveraging the power of automation, traders can enhance their profitability while staying ahead in the ever-evolving world of cryptocurrency trading. As always, balance automation with vigilance to maximize its potential while safeguarding your investments.

Chapter Nine

Building a Long-Term Crypto Investment Portfolio

A WELL-CONSTRUCTED LONG-TERM CRYPTO portfolio can offer stability, growth, and resilience against market volatility. Unlike short-term trading strategies that focus on quick profits, long-term investing prioritizes sustainable wealth accumulation by focusing on high-quality assets, diversification, and disciplined decision-making. In this chapter, we'll explore how to balance stability and growth in your portfolio and evaluate coins and projects to maximize long-term returns.

Balancing Stability and Growth

Balancing stability and growth is a cornerstone of building a robust crypto investment portfolio. This approach ensures that while a portion of your portfolio is anchored in safer, more established assets, you also capture growth opportunities in high-risk altcoins and emerging sectors.

Using Stablecoins, High-Risk Coins, and Altcoins

1. **Stablecoins for Stability** – Stablecoins like USDT (Tether), USDC (USD Coin), and DAI are pegged to fiat currencies, providing a safe haven during volatile markets. Holding a portion of your portfolio in stablecoins helps:
    - Preserve capital during market downturns.
    - Provide liquidity for buying dips or staking in DeFi protocols.
    - Generate passive income through yield farming or lending.
2. **High-Risk Coins for Growth** – High-risk coins, including new altcoins or those with smaller market caps, offer exponential growth potential but come with significant risks. Examples include emerging Layer 1 blockchains, DeFi tokens, or GameFi projects. These coins can yield high returns but require:
    - Thorough research.
    - Small allocation (e.g., 10-20% of your portfolio).
    - Regular performance monitoring to mitigate risks.
3. **Altcoins for Diversification** – Altcoins such as Ethereum (ETH), Cardano (ADA), and Polygon (MATIC) are less volatile

than high-risk coins but offer substantial growth potential. These coins typically fall into categories like Layer 1 blockchains or DeFi ecosystems, making them valuable for diversification.

Benefits of a Diversified Portfolio

A diversified portfolio is critical for mitigating risk and ensuring consistent growth. By spreading your investments across different asset categories and narratives, you reduce the impact of poor performance in any single asset.

1. **Risk Reduction** – Diversification minimizes the impact of volatility in one sector. For example, if high-risk altcoins experience a sharp decline, stablecoins and established altcoins can buffer your portfolio.

2. **Capturing Growth** – By including a mix of established altcoins and emerging projects, you position your portfolio to capitalize on both steady growth and high-risk opportunities.

3. **Long-Term Resilience** – Diversified portfolios are more likely to withstand market downturns and recover quickly during bull markets. Example Allocation:

    - 40% Bitcoin (BTC) and Ethereum (ETH): Stability and long-term growth.

    - 20% Stablecoins: Liquidity and risk mitigation.

    - 30% Altcoins (ADA, MATIC, AVAX): Growth and diversification.

- 10% High-Risk Coins (AI tokens, GameFi projects): High-growth opportunities.

Evaluating Coins and Projects

Selecting the right coins and projects is essential for building a successful long-term portfolio. This involves conducting thorough research, analyzing market trends, and assessing the viability of projects.

Researching Potential Projects

1. **Study the Fundamentals** – The foundation of any good investment decision lies in understanding the fundamentals of the project. Consider:
    - Use Case: Does the project solve a real-world problem?
    - Team: Is the development team experienced and transparent?
    - Technology: Does the project have innovative or unique features?
2. **Analyze Tokenomics** – Tokenomics refers to the economic design of the cryptocurrency. Evaluate:
    - Supply: Is the supply limited or inflationary?
    - Utility: What is the token used for within the ecosystem?

- Distribution: Are tokens fairly distributed, or do a few wallets hold most of the supply?

3. **Review Market Trends** – Pay attention to trends and narratives driving the market. For example:
   - The DeFi boom of 2020.
   - The rise of NFTs in 2021.
   - The AI narrative in 2023.

Assessing Viability

To assess whether a project is viable for long-term investment, consider these factors:

1. **Development Activity** – Active development is a strong indicator of a project's growth potential. Check:
   - GitHub repositories for updates.
   - Roadmaps for future milestones.
   - Community engagement on platforms like Discord and Twitter.
2. **Partnerships and Integrations** – Projects with strong partnerships or integrations with established players are more likely to succeed. For example:

  - Polygon's partnerships with major corporations like Disney and Starbucks.
  - Chainlink's integration with DeFi platforms for price feeds.

3. **Adoption Metrics** – Evaluate metrics like Total Value Locked (TVL) in DeFi projects, daily active users in GameFi projects, or the number of wallet addresses holding the token.

Periodic Review and Rebalancing

Building a long-term crypto portfolio is not a "set it and forget it" process. Markets evolve, technologies advance, and personal financial goals shift. Periodic review and rebalancing are essential to maintain alignment with your objectives and ensure your portfolio adapts to changing market dynamics.

Importance of Adapting to Market Changes

The cryptocurrency market is dynamic, characterized by rapid innovation, emerging trends, and volatility. A portfolio that performs well today might underperform tomorrow if not periodically reviewed and adjusted.

Why Adaptation Matters:

1. Market Cycles: Crypto markets often follow four-year cycles linked to Bitcoin halving events. As the market transitions from bull to bear phases, asset performance and risk profiles change.

2. Emerging Narratives: New sectors like DeFi, AI tokens, or GameFi can reshape the market. Staying updated ensures you're not left behind.

3. Mitigating Risks: High-performing assets may become overrepresented in your portfolio, increasing risk. Rebalancing reduces overexposure to volatile assets.

Realigning with Goals over Time

Long-term investment goals can change due to shifts in personal circumstances, market conditions, or risk tolerance. Regular portfolio reviews help you stay aligned with these goals.

Steps to Realign Your Portfolio:

1. **Reassess Your Risk Tolerance:**
    - A younger investor may allocate more to high-growth altcoins, while a retiree might prioritize stablecoins and Bitcoin for security.
    - Example: Transitioning from a growth-focused portfolio to a more conservative allocation as you approach financial milestones like buying a house or retiring.

2. **Monitor Asset Performance:**
    - Identify underperforming assets and consider reallocating funds to better-performing sectors.

- Example: If a high-risk altcoin consistently underperforms, reinvest those funds into more stable assets like Ethereum or Polygon.

3. **Incorporate New Opportunities:**
   - Emerging technologies or narratives (e.g., AI tokens like Fetch.ai (FET) or tokenized real-world assets) might align with your updated goals.
   - Periodic reviews allow you to integrate these opportunities while staying diversified.

Practical Tips for Periodic Review and Rebalancing

1. **Set a Schedule:**
   - Review your portfolio every 3-6 months or after significant market events.
   - Consistent reviews ensure you're proactively addressing shifts rather than reacting to crises.
2. **Analyze Allocation:**
   - Use tools like CoinMarketCap, Zerion, or DeFi Pulse to track asset performance and portfolio balance.

3. **Rebalance Based on Performance:**
    - If Bitcoin grows from 40% to 60% of your portfolio, sell a portion and reinvest in altcoins or stablecoins to restore balance.
4. **Stay Updated on Market Trends:**
    - Follow reputable sources, research reports, and community discussions to identify emerging opportunities.

Conclusion

Periodic review and rebalancing are vital to maintain a healthy, growth-oriented portfolio. By staying vigilant to market changes and aligning your investments with your evolving goals, you can navigate the volatility of the crypto market with confidence and consistency. Remember, the key to long-term success lies in discipline, adaptability, and a commitment to your financial objectives.

Chapter Ten

Avoiding Scams and Protecting Your Crypto Assets

THE CRYPTO SPACE OFFERS immense opportunities, but it's not without risks. With the rapid rise of digital assets, scammers have devised increasingly sophisticated methods to exploit unsuspecting investors. Protecting your crypto assets requires vigilance, awareness, and the implementation of security best practices. This chapter focuses on recognizing common scams and securing your investments.

A Common Scam and Its Impact

In 2021, a fake Initial Coin Offering (ICO) for a token called BitConnectX promised astronomical returns to early investors. Thousands of people poured millions of dollars into the project, only for it to vanish overnight. Investors lost their funds, and the scam highlighted how even seasoned traders could fall victim to fraudulent schemes. Stories like these underscore the importance of understanding scams and protecting your assets in the crypto world.

Recognizing Common Scams in Crypto

The first step to safeguarding your investments is to recognize the tactics scammers use to lure victims. Understanding these scams helps you avoid their traps.

Ponzi Schemes

Ponzi schemes involve promising high returns with little to no risk by using funds from new investors to pay earlier investors. Eventually, these schemes collapse when they can no longer attract new victims.

Example:The infamous BitConnect project lured investors with promises of daily returns of up to 1%. When the scheme collapsed in 2018, it caused billions of dollars in losses.

Signs of a Ponzi Scheme

- Guaranteed high returns with no risk.
- Pressure to recruit others to "invest."
- Lack of transparency about how profits are generated.

Fake ICOs (Initial Coin Offerings)

Fake ICOs exploit the hype around new tokens, asking investors to send funds in exchange for tokens that either don't exist or have no value.

How to Spot a Fake ICO:

- No clear roadmap or whitepaper.
- Anonymous team with no verifiable credentials.
- Unrealistic claims about future returns.

Phishing Scams

Phishing scams trick individuals into providing their private keys or login credentials through fake websites, emails, or messages.

How Phishing Works:

1. You receive an email claiming to be from your wallet provider or exchange, asking you to log in via a provided link.
2. The link directs you to a fake website that steals your credentials.
3. Scammers then access your wallet and transfer your funds.

Red Flags:

- Emails with urgent or threatening language.
- URLs that are slightly misspelled or altered.

- Requests for private keys or passwords.

Signs of a Crypto Scam

Regardless of the scam type, there are common red flags to watch for:

1. Unrealistic Promises: Guarantees of high, risk-free returns are a major warning sign.
2. Pressure Tactics: Scammers often create a sense of urgency to rush decisions.
3. Lack of Transparency: Legitimate projects are transparent about their team, technology, and goals.
4. Suspicious Communication: Official organizations won't ask for private keys or personal information.

Using Security Best Practices

Once you recognize a scam, the next step is to secure your crypto assets. This involves using secure wallets, safeguarding private keys, and choosing reliable platforms for trading.

Wallet Security

Your wallet is the gateway to your crypto assets. Proper wallet management is crucial to keep your funds safe.

Types of Wallets:

1. Hardware Wallets: Physical devices like Ledger or Trezor offer the highest level of security, as they store your private keys offline.

2. Software Wallets: Apps like MetaMask or Trust Wallet are convenient but require additional precautions to protect against hacks.

3. Cold Wallets: Offline wallets that are not connected to the internet, providing enhanced security against online threats.

Best Practices for Wallet Security:

- Backup Your Seed Phrase: Write down your wallet's recovery phrase and store it in a secure, offline location.

- Enable Two-Factor Authentication (2FA): Use 2FA for wallets and exchanges to add an extra layer of security.

- Avoid Public Wi-Fi: Don't access your wallet on unsecured networks.

Safeguarding Private Keys

Private keys are the most critical aspect of your wallet. If someone gains access to your private keys, they control your funds.

Rules for Protecting Private Keys:

1. Never Share Them: No legitimate organization will ask for your private keys.

2. Store Offline: Keep private keys on paper or a hardware wallet,

away from digital threats.

3. Use Encrypted Storage: If you must store keys digitally, ensure they are encrypted.

Choosing Safe Exchanges

Exchanges are essential for buying, selling, and trading crypto. However, not all exchanges are created equal, and choosing a secure one is paramount.

What to Look For in an Exchange:

- Regulatory Compliance: Exchanges like Coinbase and Kraken adhere to regulatory standards, offering greater security.
- Insurance Policies: Some exchanges offer insurance to cover losses from breaches.
- Security Features: Ensure the exchange uses advanced security measures like multi-signature wallets and withdrawal whitelisting.

Importance of Secure Wallets

Secure wallets act as a shield against theft and unauthorized access. By using reliable wallets and following security best practices, you reduce the risk of losing your assets to scams or hacking attempts.

Example:

In 2020, an investor using a poorly secured software wallet lost over $50,000 in Ethereum to a phishing attack. Switching to a hardware wallet would have prevented the loss.

Avoiding scams and protecting your crypto assets requires vigilance, education, and the implementation of robust security measures. By learning to recognize scams like Ponzi schemes, fake ICOs, and phishing, and adopting best practices for wallet security and exchange selection, you can navigate the crypto market with confidence. Remember, in the world of digital assets, security is your responsibility—protect your investments and stay one step ahead of potential threats.

In 2020, an investor using a poorly secured software wallet lost over $500,000 in cryptocurrency to a phishing attack. Switching to a hardware wallet would have prevented the loss.

[illegible] and [illegible] your crypto [illegible] requires [illegible] [illegible]

Chapter Eleven

Conclusion

THROUGHOUT THIS BOOK, WE'VE journeyed through the strategies and advanced techniques necessary to thrive in the dynamic world of cryptocurrency trading and investing. From building the right mindset to mastering technical analysis, developing a balanced portfolio, and safeguarding your assets, you now have a comprehensive roadmap to navigate the crypto market with confidence and clarity.

Summary

The chapters in this book were designed to build on each other, providing you with a well-rounded approach to crypto investing:

- Mindset and Psychology: Success in crypto trading starts with emotional discipline and a long-term vision. By managing fear, greed, and impulsive decisions, you can make data-driven investments rather than emotionally charged mistakes.

- Market Fundamentals and Sentiment: Understanding the market's cyclical nature, including the Bitcoin halving driven four-year cycle, equips you to anticipate trends and make informed decisions.

- Technical Analysis and Strategy Development: With tools like candlestick patterns, RSI, and moving averages, you can interpret market movements and refine personalized strategies for achieving your financial goals.

- Portfolio Building and Risk Management: A diversified portfolio of stablecoins, Layer 1 blockchains, DeFi projects, and emerging narratives provides stability and growth potential while minimizing risks.

- Passive Income and Advanced Trading: Techniques like staking, yield farming, and algorithmic trading allow you to grow your portfolio even during market downturns.

- Security and Scam Prevention: Protecting your assets from scams, hacks, and human error ensures the longevity of your investments.

Next Steps

1. Start Small and Gradually Expand: Apply what you've learned step-by-step. Begin with manageable investments, test strategies, and refine your approach as you gain experience.

2. Stay Informed: The crypto market evolves rapidly. Keep up with new trends, technological advancements, and regulatory changes to stay ahead.

3. Revisit and Adjust: Regularly review your portfolio, strategies, and risk management techniques to ensure they align with your evolving goals and market conditions.

Inspiration

Your journey into cryptocurrency is about more than just profits—it's about building a path toward financial independence and personal growth. The knowledge and tools you've gained through this book can empower you to seize opportunities in one of the most exciting financial landscapes of our time. Whether you're an aspiring investor or an experienced trader, the crypto market rewards those who combine preparation, patience, and a willingness to adapt.

Embrace the process with confidence, knowing that each step you take brings you closer to achieving your financial goals. The road to success in crypto may be challenging, but with the right mindset and strategy, the rewards can be transformative.

As you move forward, remember: your success in cryptocurrency is not just about timing the market; it's about time in the market. Stay committed, stay curious, and let this be the beginning of a journey that shapes not only your portfolio but your future.

Chapter Twelve

References

Books

AMMOUS, S. (2018). *THE Bitcoin standard: The decentralized alternative to central banking*. Wiley.

Antonopoulos, A. M. (2017). *Mastering Bitcoin: Unlocking digital cryptocurrencies*. O'Reilly Media.

Burniske, C., & Tatar, J. (2017). *Cryptoassets: The innovative investor's guide to Bitcoin and beyond*. McGraw-Hill Education.

Drescher, D. (2017). *Blockchain basics: A non-technical introduction in 25 steps*. Apress.

Diedrich, H. (2016). *Ethereum: Blockchains, digital assets, smart contracts, decentralized autonomous organizations*. Wildfire Publishing.

Lewis, R. (2020). *The basics of bitcoins and blockchains: An introduction to cryptocurrencies and the technology that powers them*. Mango Publishing.

Mougayar, W. (2016). *The business blockchain: Promise, practice, and application of the next internet technology*. Wiley.

Tapscott, D., & Tapscott, A. (2016). *Blockchain revolution: How the technology behind Bitcoin is changing money, business, and the world*. Portfolio Penguin.

Websites

Bitcoin Magazine. (2022, June 14). The history of Bitcoin: From white paper to global adoption.

Bambrough, B. (2021, February 12). Tim Draper says Bitcoin could hit $250,000 in 2022. Forbes.

Blockchaincentre.net (2025). Bitcoin Rainbow Chart.

CoinDesk. (2023, March 1). Crypto market sentiment: Tools and strategies to measure.

Cointelegraph. (2025, January 6) MicroStrategy kicks off 2025 with 1,070 Bitcoin purchase announcement.

CNBC. (2014, July 31). Tim Draper buys 30,000 Bitcoins for $19 million at U.S. auction. CNBC.https://www.cnbc.com/2014/07/31/venture-capitalist-tim-draper-buys-30000-bitcoin-at-us-auction.html

Glassnode. (2023). On-chain metrics for crypto trading.

McCaskill, S. (2021, January 11). Tim Draper on Bitcoin's future: 'Bitcoin will replace the dollar'. The Guardian.

NY Post. (2024, December 1) Crypto investors are reaping the rewards of the 'Trump Bump' and spending big on jets, cars and watches to celebrate'. NY Post.

Price, M. (2020, November 10). Tim Draper: Bitcoin will replace the dollar. Business Insider.https://www.businessinsider.com/tim-draper-says-bitcoin-will-replace-the-dollar-2020-11

Videos

Antonopoulos, A. M. (2021). *Introduction to Bitcoin and Open Blockchains* [Video]. YouTube.

Pomp Podcast. (2022). The future of DeFi and Web3. Hosted by Anthony Pompliano.

Made in the USA
Monee, IL
03 November 2026

67385906R00098